ON WORLD-GOVERNMENT

(*De Monarchia*)

The Library of Liberal Arts
OSKAR PIEST, FOUNDER

ON WORLD-GOVERNMENT

(*De Monarchia*)

DANTE ALIGHIERI

Translated by

HERBERT W. SCHNEIDER

Professor of Philosophy, Claremont Graduate School

with an introduction by

DINO BIGONGIARI

Da Ponte Professor Emeritus of Italian
Columbia University

· ·

The Library of Liberal Arts

published by

THE BOBBS-MERRILL COMPANY, INC.
INDIANAPOLIS · NEW YORK

Dante Alighieri: 1265-1321

CONTENTS
· · · · · · · · · · · · · · · ·

ON WORLD-GOVERNMENT

BOOK ONE: THAT MANKIND NEEDS UNITY AND PEACE

BOOK TWO: THAT ROMAN WORLD-RULE WAS ACQUIRED BY RIGHT

BOOK THREE: THAT TEMPORAL WORLD-RULE CAME DIRECT FROM GOD AND NOT FROM THE PAPACY

TRANSLATOR'S PREFACE

Dante intended this essay to be useful to posterity as well as to his own time. No reader of even a few of its trenchant lines can escape the impression that in this book Dante is speaking to us as well as to his contemporaries; his basic intellectual and political problems are ours. They are again basic, as they were in his day; more basic than during the intervening centuries, when the practical needs and programs of European peoples carried them off into other directions and bent their energies less toward peace than toward expansion. Dante's world imperialism, if it may be called imperialism at all, is clearly not expansive but pacific. The same might be said for his philosophy of the church. But in his day he spoke to deaf ears and seemed to be not a major prophet, but a lover of political antiques. The rising powers of guilds, trading companies, popes, and kingdoms made this sermon on world-government seem irrelevant and antiquated.

Today, however, Dante's ideal, if not his arguments, seems intensely relevant and practical. No one can read it with indifference. There is no need, accordingly, to defend a new translation made for today's political thinking rather than for students of Dante. Two notable English translations have been made, one by F. J. Church in 1879 and the other by P. H. Wicksteed in 1904. In addition to these English translations, the Italian translation and notes by Natale Vianello (1921) have been helpful in preparing this translation. The Latin text used was the edition by E. Rostagno, Florence, 1921.

The date of composition of *De Monarchia* has long been a subject of learned disagreement. A tradition going back to Boccaccio's *Life of Dante* assigns this work to the period of the expedition of Henry VII of Luxembourg into Italy, 1310-1313. However, if the reference to the *Paradiso* in I:12 is genuine, it must have been composed after 1317 and would then represent,

as it were, Dante's political and philosophical last testament.
The majority of scholars regard this reference to the *Divine
Comedy* as a gloss, and are inclined to assign an earlier date.
Undoubtedly the work comes from the period of Dante's exile
from Florence (after the triumph of the Papal Guelphs in
1301), and whether or not it was campaign literature for Henry
VII, it reflects the author's disgust at both papal policy and the
Italian princes; and whether it was written as a final protest
against both the Blacks and the Whites, in an attitude of
despair for Italian peace, or whether it reflects a passionate hope
and faith in the possibility of world peace, it comes to us as a
classic philosophical exposition of the relation between divine
and human world-government and of the relation between temporal and spiritual power. Dante's chief arguments on these
themes are summarized in the following introductory analysis
by Professor Dino Bigongiari, to whose help and instruction the
translator wishes to express his deep indebtedness.

HERBERT W. SCHNEIDER

COLUMBIA UNIVERSITY
July, 1949

INTRODUCTION

Dante's political doctrine consists of three fundamental theses.

I. The world should be united under one sovereign rule, all the various kingdoms and republics to be politically made subordinate to it.

This is the old cosmopolitanism of the Stoics revised to suit Christian needs and fitted into an Aristotelian system. The multiplicity of states, Dante holds, vying with one another for prestige and economic aggrandizement, is the source of unending woes, all of which would disappear if these states were made subordinate to one ruler strong enough to keep them in order, and devoid by reason of his status of any possible ambition, further aggrandizement no longer being possible. The universal empire is thus the only rule which insures justice. It also guarantees liberty. For the world-ruler alone, in the exercise of his power, is able to do away with the corrupt forms of government (tyranny, oligarchy, ochlocracy) and to replace them with the right regimes (kingly rule, aristocracy, and genuine democracy, that is, *politeia*). In so doing he makes it possible for peoples to be free, inasmuch as it is the lack of freedom that characterizes the corrupt political forms, each one of them subordinating the welfare and freedom of its people to the interests of a ruling group.

The basic principle, however, which controls all Dante's arguments for the necessity of a supernational government is the following: Humanity has a certain task to perform. It should actualize all that the human intellect is capable of; to produce, that is, all the arts and sciences which God meant man to work out. It is obvious that this cultural task can not be carried out by a short-lived individual, nor by a city, nor even by a kingdom, all of them limited and subject to destruction. What is needed to produce *human* culture is the collective effort of *all* humanity properly co-ordinated, unimpeded by warfare and other forms of strife. To avoid such strifes a single, supernational sovereignty is needed.

Dante here revives the old Stoic argument for the political unity of mankind, deduced from the fact of man's common possession, everywhere, of a rational faculty. But this universal *intellectus possibilis* not only takes the place of the *ratio* of Cicero and of Marcus Aurelius, it suggests the cultural actualization of what is reasonably possible. Moreover, Augustine's grand conception of *peace* as the justification of *all* political regimes serves as the capstone of a theory of humanity properly organized for its universal task. The world should therefore constitute one single state. Each one of us is a *civis* of the universal *communitas,* which is fittingly called by Dante *humana civilitas.*

II. The second fundamental principle of Dante is the independence of the head of this universal state from any political control on the part of the Church or the head thereof. The universal monarchy must be a lay state, of a kind.

Dante refutes very much in the usual way the arguments adduced by ecclesiastical opponents to such a state: the argument from the donation of Constantine, from the utterings of Christ about "two swords," his command "feed my sheep," etc. His positive argument for the political autonomy of the state is the following: man aspires to two beatitudes, one on earth, the other in heaven. The former is reached through the exercise of the moral and intellectual virtues; the other by the gift of the theological virtues. The rule over man as he strives toward the first beatitude is assigned by God himself to the Emperor; his guidance as he moves toward the second is entrusted to the Pope.

The task, thus, of the Emperor is an extraordinary one. He is responsible for keeping in line all of mankind and preventing any deviations. Since mankind is varied and lives under different conditions, the Emperor must know much of the natural order of the world in order that he may politically rule it. He must be, as Plato said, a "philosopher king." He must have the necessary *philosophica documenta.* How is he going to be so equipped? God provides: for neither God nor nature ever *de-*

ficiunt in necessariis, and this world-wide government is a *necessarium.* So there must be in the world at all times a man divinely equipped to be a universal Emperor in that he is fully conversant with the celestial causes that produce the various conditions here below which a ruler must take in consideration if he is to do his work well. How is such a man to be found? God elects him, for He is the sole Elector; the so-called electors are merely mouthpieces of his Divine Providence. The electors will receive the proper inspiration as to the choice of the Emperor if they do not let greed and covetousness cloud their minds. And as God really elects the Emperor, so does He also confirm him— He alone, not the people nor the Pope.

We thus see that Dante in supporting his conviction of the necessity of a world-rule falls back upon the fiction of divine inspiration, so often resorted to in elections whether by reliance on chance, as in antiquity, or on spiritual visitation, as among Christians.

III. The third point is more difficult. This lay universal Empire is and must remain Roman. What did Dante mean? Obviously he had in mind some such conditions as those which obtain in the Church. Just as the *ecclesia universalis* is Roman Catholic, so should the *imperium* be *Romanum.* This *imperium* must be governed by Roman law (the *Corpus Iuris* of Justinian) for that code is not man-made; it is a holy book given, or rather dictated, to man by God.

His fundamental argument is that the old Roman Empire was constituted and guided directly by God. Unlike other states, where developments took place by God's permission, the Roman Empire grew by God's direct operation. All the Roman conquests therefore were the result not of power but of justice. The Roman Empire grew *de jure,* by God's will, God showing his predilection even by the way he turned the fortunes of war; wars being in reality duels by which the judgment of God was being inquired into.

So the Empire began and so it was continued under Christian rulers and so it must go on till the end of time. We still have, Dante reminds us, the divinely inspired laws of the Roman

Corpus Iuris. With these laws, if enforced by the divinely appointed ruler, the world will do its work in peace and man will reach his earthly beatitude.

This infatuation for Rome took a humanistic turn that often verged on a repudiation of Christianity. Dante tells us at the close of Book I that mankind never was nor will it ever be as perfect as it was under the reign of Augustus. When in the Divine Comedy he comes to distinguish the good from the bad, a strange *racism* appears which seems to rout all Christian belief. The Florentines, he tells us, are partly good, partly bad. The good are those who descended from the old pagan Romans; the bad are they whose progenitors were the people of Fiesole.

What could Dante mean by this surviving Romanism? Surely he would not favor a solution occasionally discussed by jurists as to whether the ruler of the world should be elected by the then inhabitants of Rome. For the Romans of his day Dante had nothing but contempt. What counted for him was the ancient city as it survived under Christian dispensation; he hoped for the restoration of the old Roman virtues, the return of the old Roman prestige. Thus there is much Humanism or Classicism in this political doctrine. What inflames him is the love of Ancient Rome, pagan though it had been. It must be revived, in all its glory, but as the capital of the World, not as an Italian city. Italy must abandon its nationalistic aspirations, must accept its position as part of a world empire. Its revolts against Frederick I and his grandson Frederick II show how twisted its policies had been. Italy will again be great, yes! but only as the "Garden of the Empire."

DINO BIGONGIARI

Columbia University
June, 1949

SELECTED BIBLIOGRAPHY

In addition to the editions and translations mentioned in the Preface three others are noteworthy:

The Latin text edited by Edward Moore, with an introduction on political theories by H. V. Reade. Oxford, 1916.

A French translation by B. Landry with a substantial introduction. Paris, 1933.

An English translation and introduction by Donald Nicholl. London, 1955.

The chief works dealing specifically with the DE MONARCHIA *are:*

Ercole, Francesco, *Il Pensiero Politico di Dante.* 2 vols. Milan, 1927–28.

Kelsen, Hans, *Die Staatslehre des Dante Alighieri.* Vienna and Leipzig, 1905.

Kern, Fritz, *Humana Civilitas.* Leipzig, 1913.

Nardi, Bruno, "Il Concetto dell'Impero nello Svolgimento del Pensiero Dantesco," in *Giornale Storico della Letteratura Italiana,* Vol. LXXVIII. 1921.

Rivière, J., *Le problème de l'église et de l'état au temps de Philippe le Bel.* Paris, 1926.

Solmi, Arrigo, *Il Pensiero Politico di Dante.* Florence, 1922.

D'Entrèves, A. P., *Dante as a Political Thinker.* Oxford, 1952.

NOTE ON THE TEXT

The spelling of Latin words accords with Dante's own usage as reprinted in the Latin-Italian edition of 1946, edited by Angelo Camillo Volpe for the Istituto di Filologia Romanza della R. Universitá di Roma.

The headings in italics at the beginnings of Books and Chapters have been supplied by the translator for the convenience of the reader.

The translation is not "free" but follows Dante's text scrupulously. The only liberty taken by the translator in his attempt to convey Dante's meaning to modern readers is to use the impersonal term "government" in place of the antiquated terms "prince" or "emperor," when Dante is clearly referring not to a person but to "sovereign rule."

H. W. S.

ON WORLD-GOVERNMENT

ON WORLD-GOVERNMENT

BOOK ONE

THAT MANKIND NEEDS UNITY
AND PEACE

1

*The knowledge of a single temporal government over man-
kind is most important and least explored.*

All men whose higher nature has endowed them with a love
of truth obviously have the greatest interest in working for posterity, so that in return for the patrimony provided for them
by their predecessors' labors they may make provision for the
patrimony of future generations. Certainly a man who has received public instruction would be far from performing his
duty if he showed no concern for the public weal, for he would
not be a "tree by the streams of waters, bearing his fruit in due
season," but rather an erosive whirlpool always sucking in and
never returning what it devours. Therefore, as I have often re-
minded myself of these things and wish not to be charged with
burying my talent, I endeavor not only to grow in public use-
fulness but also to bear fruit by publishing truths that have not
been attempted by others. For what fruit is there in proving
once more a theorem in Euclid, or in trying to show man his
true happiness, which Aristotle has already shown, or in defending old age as Cicero did? Fruitless and positively tiresome are
such superfluous "works."

Among the truths that remain hidden, though useful, the
knowledge of the temporal government of the world is most
useful and most unknown, but since this knowledge is not directly gainful it has been neglected by all. I therefore propose

to drag it from its hiding place, in order that my alertness may be useful to the world and may bring me the glory of being the first to win this great prize. It is a difficult task I attempt and beyond my powers, but I rely not on my own ability; I trust in that giver of light who gives abundantly to all and reproaches none.

2

Since this theory is a practical science, its first principle is the goal of human civilization, which must be one and the same for all particular civilizations.

First, we must see what is meant by the temporal government of the world, both its kind and its aim. By the temporal government of the world or universal empire we mean a single government over all men in time, that is, over and in all things which can be measured by time. On this subject there are three chief questions to be examined: first, we must ask and inquire whether such a government is necessary for the good of the world; secondly, whether the Roman people has a right to assume such an office; and thirdly, whether the authority of this government comes directly from God or through some servant or vicar of God.

Since any truth which is not itself a principle is demonstrated as following from the truth of some principle, it is necessary in any inquiry to make clear from what principle the certainty of the subordinate propositions may be analytically derived. And since this treatise is an inquiry, we must first of all look for the principle on whose validity the derived propositions rest.

Now it is important to remember that there are some things entirely beyond our control, about which we can reason but do nothing, such as mathematics, physics, and theology, and there are others within our control not only for reasoning but for practice. In the latter case, action is not for the sake of thought, but thought for the sake of action, since in such matters the aim is action. Since our present concern is with politics, with the very source and principle of all right politics, and since all political matters are in our control, it is clear that our present concern is not aimed primarily at thought but at action. And furthermore, since in matters of action the final goal is the principle and cause of all, for by it the agent is first moved, it follows that any reasons for actions directed to this goal must be themselves derived from it. For example, the way to cut wood for building a house is different from the way to cut wood for a ship. Whatever, then, is the universal goal of human civilization, if there be such a goal, will serve as a first principle and will make sufficiently clear all the derivative propositions that follow. Now it would be foolish to admit that one civilization may have one goal, and another, another, and not to admit one goal for all.

3

This goal is proved to be the realization of man's ability to grow in intelligence.

Accordingly, we must now see what the whole of human civilization aims at; with this aim before us more than half our work is done, as the Philosopher says in his *Nicomachean Ethics*. And as evidence for what we seek we ought to note that just as nature makes the thumb for one purpose, the whole hand for another, the arm for still another, and the whole man for a purpose different from all these, so an individual man has one purpose, a family another, a neighborhood another, a city another, a state another, and finally there is another for all of mankind, established by the Eternal God's art, which is nature. This goal it is that we are now seeking as the guiding principle of our inquiry. We should know, in this connection, that God and nature make nothing in vain, and that whatever is produced serves some function. For the intention of any act of creation, if it is really creative, is not merely to produce the existence of something but to produce the proper functioning of that existence. Hence a proper functioning does not exist for the sake of the being which functions, but rather the being exists for the sake of its function. There is therefore some proper

function for the whole of mankind as an organized multitude
which can not be achieved by any single man, or family, or
neighborhood, or city, or state. What that may be would be
plain if we could see what the basic capacity of the whole of
humanity is. Now I would say that no capacity which several
different species have in common can be the basic power of any
one of them. For in that case the basic capacity, which characterizes a species, would be the same for several species, which is
impossible. Accordingly, man's basic power is not mere being,
for he shares being with the elements; nor is it to be compounded, for this is found in minerals, too; nor is it to be alive,
for so are plants; nor is it to be sensitive, for other animals share
this power; but it is to be sensitive to intellectual growth, for
this trait is not found in beings either above or below man. For
though there are angelic beings that share intellect with man,
they do not have intellectual growth, since their very being is
to be intellect and nothing else and hence they are intellectual
continuously, otherwise they would not be changeless. Therefore, it is clear that man's basic capacity is to have a potentiality
or power for being intellectual. And since this power can not
be completely actualized in a single man or in any of the particular communities of men above mentioned, there must be a multitude in mankind through whom this whole power can be actualized; just as there must be a multitude of created beings to
manifest adequately the whole power of prime matter, otherwise there would have to be a power distinct from prime matter, which is impossible. With this judgment Averroes agrees in
his commentary on *De anima*. This intellectual power of
which I am speaking is directed not only toward universals or
species, but also by a sort of extension toward particulars.
Hence it is commonly said that the speculative intellect becomes practical by extension, and acquires thus the aims of
action and production. I distinguish between matters of action
which are governed by political prudence, and matters of production which are governed by the arts; but all of them are
extensions of theoretical intellect, which is the best function

for which the Primal Goodness brought mankind into being. Now we have already thrown light on that saying in the *Politics* —that the intellectually vigorous naturally govern others.

4

The best means toward this end is universal peace.

I have now made clear enough that the proper work of mankind taken as a whole is to exercise continually its entire capacity for intellectual growth, first, in theoretical matters, and, secondarily, as an extension of theory, in practice. And since the part is a sample of the whole, and since individual men find that they grow in prudence and wisdom when they can sit quietly, it is evident that mankind, too, is most free and easy to carry on its work when it enjoys the quiet and tranquillity of peace. Man's work is almost divine ("Thou hast made him a little lower than the angels"), and it is clear that of all the things that have been ordained for our happiness, the greatest is universal peace. Hence there rang out to the shepherds from on high the good news, not of riches, nor pleasures, nor honors, nor long life, nor health, nor strength, nor beauty, but peace. For the heavenly host proclaimed "glory to God in the highest and on earth peace to men of good will." Hence, too, "Peace be with you" was the salutation of Him who is the Salvation of men; for it was fitting that the Supreme Saviour should give voice to the supreme salutation. His disciples took care to make this salutation customary, and so did Paul in his salutations, as must be evident to all.

What I have now said makes clear what is that better, that best way, by following which mankind may achieve its proper work, and consequently it is also clear what way we must directly take to attain that final goal set for all our work, which is universal peace. Let this, then, be our principle underlying all our subsequent arguments, as I said, and let it serve as a standard set before us by which to test the truth of whatever we shall try to prove.

5

To achieve this state of universal well-being a single world-government is necessary.

There are three chief questions, as I said in the beginning, which must be raised and discussed concerning the temporal government of the world, more commonly called empire, and these three I propose, as I said, to take up in order. And so the first question is, whether a single temporal world-government is necessary for the world's well-being. There exists no weight of argument or of authority against this necessity and there are very strong and clear arguments for it. The first argument, which enjoys the authority of the Philosopher, is in his *Politics,* where this venerable authority states that whenever several things are united into one thing, one of them must regulate and rule, the others must be regulated and ruled. This seems credible not only on the strength of the glorious name of its author, but also for inductive reasons. Consider, for example, an individual man; we see this truth exhibited in him, for while all his energies are directed toward happiness, he could not attain it did not his intellectual power rule and guide the others. Or consider a household whose aim it is to prepare the members of the family to live well; one alone must regulate and rule, whom we call father of the family, or else there is someone who takes his place. So says our Philosopher: "Every home is ruled by the eldest." It is his duty, as Homer says, to govern all and give laws to others. Hence the proverbial curse: "May you have an equal in your home!" Or consider a neighborhood whose aim is to provide mutual aid in persons and things. Someone must govern the others, either someone appointed by the others or some outstanding member whom the others consent to follow, otherwise the community will not only fail to furnish the mutual aid for which it exists, but, as sometimes happens when several strive for pre-eminence, the whole neighborhood is destroyed. Likewise a city, whose aim is to live well and self-suffidently, must have a single government, whether the city have a just or corrupt constitution. Otherwise not only does civil life fail to reach its goal, but the city ceases to be what it was. Or take finally a state or kingdom, whose aim is the same as that of a city, save that it takes more responsibility for peace—there must be a single government which both rules and governs; otherwise the end of the state is lost sight of, or the state itself falls to pieces, according to the infallible truth: "Every kingdom directed against itself shall be laid waste." If, therefore, these things are true among individuals and particular communities which have a unified goal, what we proposed above must be true. Since it appears that the whole of mankind is ordained to one end, as we proved above, it should therefore have a single rule and government, and this power should be called the Monarch or Emperor. And thus it is plain that for the well-being of the world there must be a single world-rule or empire.

6

Since any particular institution needs unity of direction, mankind as a whole must also need it.

Whatever relation a part bears to its whole, the structure of that part must bear to the total structure. But a part is related to the whole as to its end or greatest good. Hence we must conclude that the goodness of the partial structure cannot exceed the goodness of the total structure, rather the contrary. Now since there is a double structure among things—namely, the structure which relates part to part, and the structure which relates parts to a whole that is not itself a part, as in any army soldiers are related to each other and also to their commander —it follows the structure which makes a unity out of parts is better than the other structure, for it *is* what the other aims at. Therefore the relations among parts exist for the sake of the unifying structure, not vice versa. Hence, if the form of this structure is found among the partial associations of men, much more should it be found in the society of men as a totality, on

the strength of the preceding syllogism, since the total structure
or its form is the greater good. But, as we have seen sufficiently
clearly in the preceding chapter, this unifying structure is found
in all parts of human society; therefore it is found or should be
found in mankind as a whole; and as those societies that are
partial in a state and the state itself, as we saw, should be composed of a structure unified by a governor or government, so
there must be a single world-ruler or world-government.[1]

7

*Human government is but a part of that single world-admin-
istration which has its unity in God.*

Furthermore, human society is a totality in relation to its
parts, but is itself a part of another totality. For it is the totality
of particular states and peoples, as we have seen, but it is obviously a mere part of the whole universe. Therefore, as through
it the lower parts of human society are well-ordered, so it, too,
should fit into the order of the universe as a whole. But its parts
are well-ordered only on the basis of a single principle (this
follows from all we have said), and hence it too must be well-
ordered on the basis of a single principle, namely, through its
governor, God, who is the absolute world-government. Hence
we conclude that a single world-government is necessary for
the well-being of the world.

8

*Man is by nature in God's likeness and therefore should, like
God, be one.*

Things are at their best when they go according to the intention of their original mover, who is God. And this is self-evident
to all except those who deny that the divine goodness achieves

1 The term "prince" and cognate terms are used by writers in the
classical tradition as a technical term for sovereign government and may
be translated impersonally.

the highest perfection. In the intention of God every creature exists to represent the divine likeness in so far as its nature makes this possible. According to what is said: "Let us make man after our image and likeness." Though we cannot speak of the divine "image" as being in things lower than man, we can speak of anything as being in His "likeness," since the whole universe is nothing but a kind of imprint of the divine goodness. Therefore, mankind exists at its best when it resembles God as much as it can. But mankind resembles God most when it is most unified, for the true ground of unity exists in Him alone, as is written: "Hear, O Israel, the Lord thy God is one." But mankind is then most one when it is unified into a single whole; which is possible only when it submits wholly to a single government, as is self-evident. Therefore mankind in submitting to a single government most resembles God and most nearly exists according to the divine intention, which is the same as enjoying well-being, as was proved at the beginning of this chapter.

9

The heavens are ruled by a single mover, God, and man is at his best when he follows the pattern of the heavens and the heavenly father.

So also a person is a good or perfect child when he follows, as far as nature permits, in the footsteps of a perfect father. But mankind is the son of heaven, which is most perfect in all its works; for "man is generated of man and sun," according to the author of *The Physics*.[2] Hence mankind is best when it follows in the footsteps of heaven as far as its nature permits. And as the whole heaven is governed in all its parts, motions, and movers by a single motion, the *primum mobile,* and by a single mover, God, as is very evident to a philosophizing reason if it syllogizes truly, it follows that mankind is then at its best when in all its movers and movements it is governed by a single mover or government and by a single motion or law. Thus it seems

[2] II. 2, 11.

necessary that for the well-being of the world there be world-government, that is, a single power, called Empire. This reasoning inspired Boethius when he said:

> O happy race of men,
> If like heaven your hearts
> Were ruled by love! [3]

10

Human governments are imperfect as long as they are **not** *subordinate to a supreme tribunal.*

Wherever there can be contention, there judgment should exist; otherwise things would exist imperfectly, without their own means of adjustment or correction, which is impossible, since in things necessary God or Nature is not defective. Between any two governments, neither of which is in any way subordinate to the other, contention can arise either through their own fault or that of their subjects. This is evident. Therefore there should be judication between them. And since neither can know the affairs of the other, not being subordinated (for among equals there is no authority), there must be a third and wider power which can rule both within its own jurisdiction. This third power is either the world-government or it is not. If it is, we have reached our conclusion; if it is not, it must in turn have its equal outside its jurisdiction, and then it will need a third party as judge, and so *ad infinitum,* which is impossible. So we must arrive at a first and supreme judge for whom all contentions are judiciable either directly or indirectly; and this will be our world-governor or emperor. Therefore, world-government is necessary for the world. The Philosopher saw this argument when he said, "Things hate to be in disorder, but a plurality of authorities is disorder; therefore, authority is single." [4]

[3] *On the Consolation of Philosophy* II.8.
[4] Quoted in Aristotle's *Metaphysics* XI.10 from Homer's *Iliad* II.204.

11

The world-government is apt to be least greedy and most just.

Moreover, the world is best ordered when justice is its greatest power. Thus Virgil, seeking to praise an age which seemed to be arising in his day, sang in his *Bucolics:*

Iam redit et Virgo, redeunt Saturnia regna.[5]

By "Virgo" he meant justice, sometimes called "the starry." By "Saturnia regna" he meant the best ages, sometimes called "the golden." Justice has greatest power under a unitary government; therefore the best order of the world demands world-government or empire. The minor premise will become evident if we recall that justice is by its nature a kind of rightness or straight rule without deviation, and therefore, like whiteness, justice in the abstract is not susceptible of degrees. For certain forms are of this kind, entering into various compounds but each being in itself single and invariable, as the author of the *Book of the Six Principles* [6] rightly says. However, when they are qualified by "more or less," they owe this qualification to the things with which they are mixed and which contain a mixture of qualities more or less incompatible. Hence wherever justice exists with the least mixture of what is incompatible with it, either in *disposition* or in *action,* there justice is most powerful. And then what the Philosopher says can truly be said of her: "She is fairer than the morning or the evening star." [7] For then she resembles Phoebe in the glow and calm of dawn facing her brother [Phoebus Apollo]. As to its *disposition,* justice is often obscured by volition, for when the will is not entirely freed of greed before justice is introduced, its justice lacks the brightness of purity, for it is mixed, however slightly, with something foreign to it; hence it is well that those be condemned

[5] "At last the Virgin and the Saturnian Kingdoms are returning."
[6] Gilbertus Porretanus.
[7] *Ethics* V. I.

who try to influence the sentiments of a judge. And as to its *action,* justice suffers from the limitations of human ability; for since justice is a virtue affecting others, how can a person act justly when he lacks the ability of giving to each his due? Whence it follows that the more powerful a just man is, the more adequate can justice be in its action.

And so, on the basis of this proposition, we may argue as follows: justice is most powerful in the world when it resides in the most willing and able being; the only being of this nature is the world-governor. Therefore, justice is the most powerful in the world when it resides solely in the world-governor. This compound syllogism is in the second figure necessarily negative, thus:

All B is A		All B is A
Only C is A	or	No non-C is A
Only C is B		No non-C is B

The major premise is evident from the foregoing. The minor is justified as follows: first, respecting *volition,* then, respecting *ability.* As evidence for the first we must note that greed is the extreme opposite of justice, as Aristotle says in the Fifth Book of his *Nicomachean Ethics.* Take away greed completely and nothing opposed to justice remains in the will. Hence the opinion of the Philosopher that whatever can be decided by law should not be left to a judge, is based on the fear of greed, which readily twists the minds of men. Now where there is nothing left to desire, greed is impossible, for passions cannot exist when their objects are destroyed. But a universal ruler has nothing that he still desires, for his jurisdiction is bounded only by the ocean, which is true of no other ruler whose realm is bounded by those of others, as, for example, the King of Castile's is bounded by the King of Aragon's. Hence it follows that the world-ruler is the purest among mortal wills in which justice may reside. Moreover, as greed, however slight, obscures the habits of justice, so charity or joy in righteousness refines and enlightens it. Whoever, therefore, is most disposed to find joy in righteousness can give to justice the greatest pre-eminence. Such is the world-ruler, and if he exist, justice is or can be most powerful. That righteous joy does what I have claimed for it can be proved as follows: greed ignores man himself and seeks other things, but charity ignores all other things and seeks God and man, and consequently man's good. And since of all human goods the greatest is to live in peace, as we said above, and since justice is its chief and most powerful promoter, charity is the chief promoter of justice—the greater charity, the more justice. And that of all men the world-ruler should most enjoy righteousness can be made clear thus: if we love a thing, we love it more the closer it is to us; but men are closer to the world-ruler than to other rulers; therefore he loves them most or should love them most. The major premise is evident to anyone who considers the nature of being passive and being active; the minor follows from the fact that men are close to other rulers only in part, but to the world-ruler totally. Also, men approach other rulers through the ruler of all, not *vice versa,* and thus all men are the primary and immediate objects of concern for the world-ruler, whereas other rulers care for them only through him from whose supreme care their own is derived. Besides, the more universal a cause is, the more genuinely it is a cause, for lower causes operate through the higher, as is explained in the book *De causis,* and the more a cause is a cause, the more it loves its effect, since such a love makes a cause what it is. Therefore, since the world-ruler is among mortals the most universal cause of well-being, other rulers being so through him, as I have explained, it follows that he has the greatest love for human welfare.

Secondly, concerning the *ability* [rather than the will] to do justice, who could doubt such an ability in the world-ruler, if he understands the meaning of the term? For since he governs all, he can have no enemies. The minor premise is now evident enough, and the conclusion seems certain—namely, that the world needs for its well-being a universal government.

12

Human freedom consists in being ruled by reason and in living for the goal of mankind. Such freedom is possible only under world-government.

Mankind is at its best when it is most free. This will be clear if we grasp the principle of liberty. We must realize that the basic principle of our freedom is freedom to choose, which saying many have on their lips but few in their minds. For they go only so far as to say freedom of choice is freedom of will in judging. This is true, but they do not understand its import. They talk as our logicians do, who for their exercises in logic constantly use certain propositions, such as "A triangle has three angles equal to two right angles." And so I must explain that judgment lies between apprehension and appetition; for, first a thing is apprehended, then, being apprehended, is judged to be good or bad, and lastly, being judged, is either sought or rejected. Therefore, if the judgment completely dominates the appetite and is in no way prejudiced by appetite, it is free; but if the appetite somehow antecedes the judgment and influences it, the judgment can not be free, since it does not move itself, but is led captive by another. For this reason, the lower animals can not have free judgment, since their appetites always get ahead of their judgments. This also explains why intellectual beings whose wills are immutable and those spirits who have departed this life in grace do not lose their freedom of judgment, though their wills are fixed, but retain and exercise it perfectly.

If we grasp this principle, we can again appreciate why this liberty, the principle of all our liberty, is God's greatest gift to human nature (as I said in the "Paradiso"),[8] for in this life it makes us happy as men, and in another it makes us happy as gods. If all this is true, who can deny that mankind lives best when it makes the most use of this principle?

8 This is probably a gloss. See Preface, p. x.

But to live under a world-ruler is to be most free. To understand this, we must know that to be free means to exist for one's own sake, not for another's, as the Philosopher puts it in his *De simpliciter ente*.[9] For whatever exists for the sake of another is under a necessity derived from that for which it exists, as a road is necessarily determined by its goal. Now it is only under the reign of a world-ruler that mankind exists for itself and not for another, since then only is there a check on perverted forms of government such as democracies, oligarchies, and tyrannies, which carry mankind into slavery, as anyone can see who runs down the list of them all, whereas those only govern who are kings, aristocrats (called "the best"), and champions of the people's liberty. Hence the world-ruler, who has the greatest love for men, as I have explained, desires that all men be made good, which is impossible among perverted politicians. Thus the Philosopher says in his *Politics* that "under a perverted form of government a good man is a bad citizen, while under a right form a good man and a good citizen are identical." In this way right forms of government aim at liberty, that is, men live for their own sake. For citizens do not live for their representatives nor peoples for their kings, but, on the contrary, representatives exist for citizens and kings for peoples. As a social order is established not for the sake of the laws, but the laws for its sake, so they who live according to law are ordered not for the sake of the legislator but rather he for them. This is the way the Philosopher puts it in his books on this subject that have come down to us. Hence it is clear that though in matters of policy representatives and kings are the rulers of others, in matters of aims they are the servants of others, and most of all the world-ruler, who should be regarded as the servant of all. Hence we must be well aware that world-government is itself governed by a pre-established end in establishing its laws. Therefore mankind lives best when it lives under a single ruler; and it follows that a single world-government is necessary for the world's well-being.

[9] *Metaphysics* I.

13

The universal government is most apt to be reasonable.

Another argument: Whoever is himself best disposed to rule
can best dispose others. For in any action what is primarily intended by the agent, either because his nature demands it or
because he does it purposely, is to make manifest his own image; hence an agent is delighted when he is thus active, for as all
things desire their own being, and as an agent in acting unfolds
his own being, a state of delight naturally arises, for a thing desired always brings delight. An agent acts, therefore, only because he already is the kind of thing which what he acts on is
supposed to become. On this subject the Philosopher says in *De
simpliciter ente*: "Whatever is changed from potentiality into
act is changed by something which actually exists in the form
to which it is changed; if an agent tried to act otherwise, he
would act in vain." And thus we can overcome the error of
those who speak well but do ill and who nevertheless believe
that they can improve the life and ways of others; they forget
that Jacob's hands were more persuasive than his words, even
though his words were true and his hands false. Hence the Philosopher says in his *Nicomachean Ethics:* "In matters of passion and action, words are less persuasive than deeds." Hence
also heaven spoke to David when he sinned, saying: "Wherefore dost thou tell of my righteousness?"—as much as to say:
"Your speech is in vain when you are not as you speak." From
all this we gather that whoever wishes to order others well
should himself be well-ordered. But it is the world-ruler alone
who is best constituted for ruling. The proof is as follows: A
thing is most easily and perfectly adapted to a given course of
action when it contains in itself few obstacles to this action.
Thus those who have never heard of philosophizing truly are
more easily and perfectly taught the habit [of it] than those who
heard of it long ago and are full of false opinions. On this subject Galen well says: "It takes such persons double time to ac-

quire science." Now since the world-ruler can have no occasion for greed, or at least has much less than other mortals, as we explained above, and since this does not apply to other rulers, and since greed is itself the great corrupter of judgment and impediment to justice, it follows that the world-ruler is wholly or to the greatest possible degree well-constituted for ruling, since he above all others can let judgment and justice hold sway. These are the two chief qualities that legislators and administrators of law should have, as that most holy king testified when he asked God to give him what a king and a king's son should have: "God give thy judgment to the king, and thy justice to the king's son." Therefore, our minor premise is sound, in which we say that the world-ruler alone has the best qualifications for ruling. Therefore, the world-ruler can best govern others. Hence it follows that for the best state of the world a world-government is necessary.

14

The universal government can best guide particular governments by establishing the laws which lead all men in common toward peace.

It is better that what can be done by one should be done by one, not by many. The demonstration of this proposition is: Let A be able to do something; let A and B be several who could also do it. Now if A can do what A and B do, B is useless, for his addition makes no difference to what A alone did. Such useless additions are superfluous and otiose, displeasing to God and Nature, and whatever is displeasing to God and Nature is evil (which is self-evident); it follows not only that it is better that one rather than many should do this work, but that it is good for one to do it and evil for several to do it.

Another proof: A thing is said to be better the nearer it is to the best. Now the end for which a deed is done is the standard of its goodness. But when it is done by one it is nearer the end. Therefore, it is better so. To prove that when it is done by one, it is nearer the end, let C be the end, let A be the deed of one, and let A and B be the deed of several. It is clear that the way from A direct to C is shorter than via B. Now mankind can be ruled by a single supreme ruler or world-governor. In this connection it should be clearly understood that not every little regulation for every city could come directly from the world-government, for even municipal regulations are sometimes defective and need amendment, as the Philosopher makes clear in his praise of equity in the *Nicomachean Ethics*. Thus nations, states, and cities have their own internal concerns which require special laws. For law is a rule to guide our lives. The Scythians must rule their lives in one way, living as they do beyond the seventh clime, suffering great inequalities of days and nights and being harried by an almost intolerable, freezing cold, whereas the Garamantes must do otherwise, living below the equinoctial circle, where daylight and dark of night are always balanced, and where the excessive heat makes clothes unendurable. World-government, on the other hand, must be understood in the sense that it governs mankind on the basis of what all have in common and that by a common law it leads all toward peace. This common norm or law should be received by local governments in the same way that practical intelligence in action receives its major premises from the speculative intellect. To these it adds its own particular minor premises and then draws particular conclusions for the sake of its action. These basic norms not only can come from a single source, but must do so in order to avoid confusion among universal principles. Moses himself followed this pattern in the law which he composed, for, having chosen the chiefs of the several tribes, he left them the lesser judgments, reserving to himself alone the higher and more general. These common norms were then used by the tribal chiefs according to their special needs. Therefore, it is better for mankind to be governed by one, not by many; and hence by a single governor, the world-ruler; and if it is better, it is pleasing to God, since He always wills the better. And when there are only two alternatives—the better is also the best, and is consequently not only pleasing to God, but the choice of "one" rather than "many" is what most pleases Him. Hence it follows that mankind lives best under a single government, and therefore that such a government is necessary for the well-being of the world.

15

Unity is basic to both "being" and "good."

Now I must explain that "being," "unity," and "good" have an order of precedence in the fifth sense of "precedence," namely, priority. For by its nature being is prior to unity and unity prior to the good, because whatever is in the fullest sense a being is most unified, and when most unified it is most good. Hence the less a thing has complete being, the less unity it has, and consequently it is less good. For this reason it is true in all matters whatsoever that the most unified is the best; so the Philosopher maintains in *De simpliciter ente*. Thus we see that at the root of what it means to be good is being one; and the root of what it means to be evil is being many. For this reason, as is explained in *De simpliciter ente*, Pythagoras in his system of relations places unity on the side of good and plurality on the side of evil. Thus we can see what sin is: it is to scorn unity and hence to proceed toward plurality. The Psalmist saw this very well when he said: "They are multiplied in the fruit of corn and wine and oil." It is therefore certain that whatever is good is good because it is unified. And since concord is essentially a good, it is clear that at its root there must be some kind of unity; what this root is will become evident if we examine the nature and ground of concord. Now concord is a uniform movement of many wills; in this definition we see that the uniform movement is due to the union of wills, and that this union is the root and very being of concord. For example, we would say that a number of clods of earth would all agree in falling toward the center and that they fell "in concord," if they did so voluntarily, and similarly flames would agree in rising to the circumference. So we speak of a number of men as being in concord when in moving together toward a single goal their wills are formally united, that is, the form of unity is in their wills, just as the quality of gravity is formally in the clods, and levity in the flames. For the ability to will is a kind of power, but the form of the will is the idea of an apprehended good. This form, like any other form (such as soul or number) is in itself a unity, but is multiplied in the various things with which it is compounded.

With this in mind we can now proceed to our argument in behalf of our proposition, as follows: All concord depends on a unity in wills; the best state of mankind is a kind of concord, for as a man is in excellent health when he enjoys concord in soul and body, and similarly a family, city, or state, so mankind as a whole. Therefore the well-being of mankind depends on the unity of its wills. But this is possible only if there is a single, dominant will which directs all others toward unity, for the wills of mortals need direction because they are subject to the captivating delights of youth (so teaches the Philosopher at the end of his *Nicomachean Ethics*). And this will can not be if there be not a single governor of all whose will can be dominant and directive for all others. Now, if all the above arguments are true, and they are, it is necessary for the best state of mankind that there be in the world a single governor, and consequently world-government is necessary for the well-being of the world.

16

The incarnation of Christ during the Augustan Empire when there prevailed a maximum of world peace bears witness that these principles are divine, and the miseries which have overtaken man since he departed from that golden age likewise bear witness.

Memorable experience confirms the above rational arguments. I refer to the state of things among mortals at the time when the Son of God took on human form for man's salvation, a state of things which He either awaited or arranged according to his will. For if we recall all the ages and conditions of men since the fall of our first parent, when the whole course of our wanderings began, we shall find that not until the time of Divus Augustus was there a complete and single world-government which pacified the world. That in his time mankind enjoyed the blessing of universal peace and tranquillity is the testimony of all historians, of the illustrious poets, and even of the evangelist of Christ's gentleness [St. Luke]; and lastly this happiest of ages was called by Paul the "fullness of time." Truly the time was full and all things temporal so ordered that for every service toward our happiness there was a servant.

But the condition of the world since the day when the nail of greed tore that seamless garment is something we can all read about, if only we did not have to see it, too! O race of men, how many storms and misfortunes must thou endure, and how many shipwrecks, because thou, beast of many heads, strugglest in many directions! Thou art sick at heart and sick in mind, both theoretical and practical! No irrefutable arguments appeal to thy theoretical reason, and no amount of experience to thy practical intelligence, and even thine emotions are not moved by the sweet, divine persuasiveness which sounds to thee from the trumpet of the Holy Spirit: "Behold how good and how pleasant it is for brethren to dwell together in unity. Why have the nations raged, and the people devised vain things? The kings of the earth stood up and the princes met together against the Lord, and against his Christ. Let us break their bonds asunder: and let us cast away their yoke from us." [10]

[10] Psalm 2:1-3.

BOOK TWO

THAT ROMAN WORLD-RULE
WAS ACQUIRED BY RIGHT

1

Both human reason and divine authority show that the Roman Empire existed by right.

We marvel at a novel effect when its cause is not apparent to us, and so those who know the cause despise and deride those who marvel. There was a time when I too marveled at the way the Roman people made itself pre-eminent throughout the world without resistance, for in my superficial view I thought that they obtained this power by force of arms and without right. But now that my mind's eye penetrates more deeply and I see the most evident sign of divine Providence behind this process, my marveling ceases, and with derision I now look down upon those nations whom I know to have raved and upon those peoples whom I see meditating vain things, as I myself used to do, and I grieve at the sight of kings and princes who can agree only in opposing their Lord and his Roman prince. And so in derision, but not without grief, I can cry out in behalf of the glorious people and of Caesar in the words of him who cried out in behalf of the Prince of Heaven: "Why have the nations raged and the peoples devised vain things? The kings of the earth stood up and the princes met together against the Lord, and against his Christ."[1] But as love naturally does not permit derision to endure, and as the summer sun in his rising scatters the morning mists and bathes all in light, so I cease deriding and prefer to throw a correcting light upon the clouds of ignorance, to free from such clouds those raving

[1] Psalm 2:1-2.

kings and princes and to reveal a mankind freed from the yoke of such rulers, and as I embark on the following argument I exhort myself in the words of the Holy Prophet: "Let us burst their chains and cast their yoke from us!"

Both of these aims will be achieved when I have completed the second part of my inquiry and tell the truth concerning this question. For in showing that the Roman Empire existed by right I shall not only remove the clouds of ignorance from the eyes of those kings and princes who are usurping the public authority and believe falsely that it was the Roman people who was the usurper, but I shall show all mortals that they are free from the yoke of these usurpers. Now this truth will be revealed not only by the light of human reason, but also by the rays of divine authority. When these two agree, heaven and earth must necessarily assent. Holding, therefore, to the faith which I have avowed and trusting in the joint testimony of reason and authority, I proceed to unravel the second question.

2

The will of God is the basis of right.

Now that we have investigated sufficiently, as far as the nature of the matter permits, what the true answer to the first question is, we must look for the truth concerning the second question, namely, whether the Roman people acquired its dignity of empire by right. Here again we must begin our inquiry by seeing what truth it is that may serve as its principle, on which the relevant arguments are grounded.

The first fact to note in this connection is that, as any art exists in a threefold manner—in the artist's mind, in the technique, and in the medium—so we must view nature as threefold. For nature is in God as its prime mover, then in the celestial bodies, which are his instruments and by which the image of his eternal goodness is manifested in the material flux or medium of his art. Given a perfect artist with perfect instruments, if the work is imperfect, the fault must lie in the medium alone.

Thus, since God achieves the highest perfection, and since his instruments, the heavens, are without defects (as we learn in philosophizing about them), only one alternative remains: any defect in things here below must be due to a defect in God's raw material, and must be external to the intention of the God of creation and of heaven. On the other hand, if we find something good here below, we can not refer it to the material itself, since the raw material is only potential art, and we must attribute any good primarily to the divine artist and secondarily to the heavenly bodies which are the instruments of God's art, commonly called nature. From this we can now infer that the right, since it is a good, exists primarily in the mind of God; and since whatever is in God's mind is God himself (according to the saying, "What was made, was life in Him"), and since God is the chief object of his own will, it follows that the right, being in God, is willed by Him. And since the will and its object are identical in God, it follows further that God's will is itself the right. Moreover it follows that whatever right exists in things is nothing other than the image of God's will. Hence, whatever does not agree with the divine will can not be right, and whatever does agree with it is right. Therefore, when we ask whether anything happens by right, we merely mean whether it happens according to the will of God, whatever other words we may use. We must accordingly suppose that whatever in human society God really wills must be regarded as truly and genuinely right. In this connection we ought to recall what the Philosopher teaches in the beginning of his *Nicomachean Ethics*: "We must not expect to find the same kind of certainty in all subjects, but according to what the nature of the subject permits." Thus our arguments will be sufficiently well grounded on the principle which we have stated, if we base the right possessed by this glorious people on the evidence of clear signs and the authority of the wise; for in itself God's will is invisible, but through visible events the mind is able to see the invisible things of God. Just as a wax impression gives clear evidence of what seal made it, though the seal itself is never seen, so we should not wonder that we must look for the divine will by visible signs, for even our human wills can be detected by others only through signs.

3

The Roman people was the noblest.

Hence my position on this question is that the Roman people acquired that unified rule over all mortals which is called "empire" by right and not by usurpation. This thesis I prove in the first place as follows: the noblest people deserves to be put above all others; the Roman people was the noblest; therefore, it should be put above all others. The major premise can be proved rationally: for, since "honor is the reward of virtue," and all preferments are honors, every preferment is a reward of virtue. But it is agreed that it is by virtue that men are ennobled, either by their own virtue or by that of their forebears. So the Philosopher says in the *Politics,* "Nobility is virtue plus ancient riches," [2] and Juvenal says, *Nobilitas animi sola est atque unica virtus.*[3] These two statements refer to two kinds of nobility, one's own and that of one's forebears. Hence it stands to reason that only the noble deserve the reward of pre-eminence. And since rewards should be according to merit, as the Gospel says, "The same measure which you have applied will be applied to you," it is fitting that to the noblest should be given the highest station.

The minor premise is held to be true according to the testimony of the ancients; for our divine poet Virgil throughout his *Aeneid* pays tribute to the everlasting memory of glorious King Aeneas as the father of the Roman people; so also Titus Livy, the distinguished historian of the Romans' achievements, devotes the first part of his book to the fall of Troy. It is needless here to expound how great was the nobility of that uncon-

2 Aristotle *Politics* IV. VIII. 9.
3 *Satires* VIII. 20. "Nobility of mind is the one and only virtue."

querable man and pious father, not only because of his own virtue, but also because by hereditary right the nobility of his line and of his spouses' lines were united in him. Suffice it to mention some of the high spots.

As to his own nobility, hear how he is introduced by our Poet in the first book of the *Aeneid* in the prayer of Ilioneus—

> *Rex erat Eneas nobis, quo iustior alter*
> *nec pietate fuit nec bello maior et armis.*[4]

Hear likewise from the sixth book where, telling about the death of Misenus, who was Hector's shield-bearer and who after Hector's death served Aeneas, he says that this Misenus "became servant to no lesser man," [5] thus equating Aeneas and Hector, whom Homer glorified above all others, as the Philosopher tells us in the passage of the *Nicomachean Ethics* in which he describes despicable traits.[6] And as to Aeneas' hereditary nobility, all three continents of the earth contributed to his and his family's nobility. For among his nearer ancestors were Assaracus and other Phrygian kings from Asia, and hence our Poet writes in the third book—

> *Postquam res Asie Priamique evertere gentem*
> *immeritam visum superis.*[7]

From Europe came his ancient ancestor Dardanus, whose earliest African ancestor was Electra, child of the famous King Atlas. To both of these our Poet bears witness in the eighth book, where Aeneas, speaking to Evander, says—

> *Dardanus Yliace primus pater urbis et auctor,*
> *Electra, ut Grai perhibent, Athlantide cretus,*
> *advehitur Teucros: Electram maximus Athlas*
> *edidit, ethereos humero qui sustinet orbes.*[8]

[4] I. 544. "Our king was Aeneas, none more just than he, nor more pious, nor greater in battle and arms."

[5] VI. 170.

[6] Aristotle *Nicomachean Ethics* Book VII. I. 1, citing Homer's *Iliad* XXIV. 258-259.

[7] III. 1. "The gods having decided to overturn the affairs of Asia and of Priam's guiltless kin."

[8] VIII. 134ff. "To Teucri came Dardanus, Ilium's first father and

This same bard sings of the European birth of Dardanus in his third book—

> *Est locus, Hesperiam Grai cognomine dicunt,*
> *terra antiqua, potens armis atque ubere glebe;*
> *Oenotri coluere viri; nunc fama minores*
> *Ytaliam dixisse ducis de nomine gentem:*
> *hee nobis proprie sedes, hinc Dardanus ortus.*[9]

That Atlas came from Africa can be inferred from the mountain there that bears his name, and that this mountain is in Africa we know from Orosius, who says in his description of the world: "Its end is Mount Atlas and the islands called Fortunate." The word "its" refers to Africa, of which he was speaking.

In a similar way Aeneas' nobility can also be traced through his marriages. His first wife was Creusa, the daughter of King Priam of Asia (as we have noted above). And our Poet testifies that she was his spouse, for in the third book, where Andromache is asking Aeneas about his son, Ascanius, she asks—

> *Quid puer Ascanius ? superatne et vescitur aura,*
> *quem tibi iam Troya peperit fumante Creusa?* [10]

His second wife was Dido, an African queen and ancestor of the Carthaginians; and our Poet in his fourth book sings of her as his spouse, for he says of Dido—

> *Nec iam furtivum Dido meditatur amorem:*
> *coniugium vocat; hoc pretexit nomine culpam.*[11]

The third wife was Lavinia, ancestor of both the Albans and Romans, daughter and heiress of King Latinus, if the testi-

---

founder of the city; he was the son of Electra, whom the Greeks called Atlantides, child of great Atlas, who bears on his shoulders the heavenly spheres."

9 III. 163ff. "There is a place called Hesperia by the Greeks, an old country, strong in arms and fertile of soil, inhabited by the Oenotrians; now, tradition has it, their descendants have named it Italy, after their leader. Here is our true home and hence came Dardanus."

10 III. 339. "And how about Ascanius? Is he alive and does he still breathe on earth, he whom Creusa bore to you in smoldering Troy?"

11 IV. 171. "And Dido no longer tried to conceal her love. She called it marriage and thus covered her guilt."

mony of our Poet in his last book is reliable, where he brings in
Turnus, conquered and suppliant, saying to Aeneas—

Vicisti, et victum tendere palmas
Ausonii videre: tua est Lavinia coniunx.[12]

This, his last wife, was from Italy, the noblest region of Europe.

With these evidences for the minor premise, who is not sufficiently persuaded that the ancestor of the Romans and hence
the Roman people itself was the noblest under heaven? And
who can fail to see in this triple unity of the blood of three
continents a sign of divine predestination?

4

Miracles attest God's care for Rome.

Secondly, whatever is accomplished with the aid of miracles
is according to God's will and hence takes place by right. The
truth of this statement is made clear by Thomas in Book III of
his treatise *Against the Gentiles,* where he says, "A miracle is
any event in the divine order which takes place outside the
common course of events." [13] Here he himself shows that God
alone can work miracles. This is confirmed by the authority of
Moses when he tells how, during the plague of locusts, the wise
men of Pharaoh, whose art is a utilization of natural principles, admitted their failure and excused themselves saying,
"Here is the finger of God." If, therefore, a miracle is the direct
operation of the First Cause without secondary agent, as
Thomas himself in the above-mentioned work abundantly
proves, it is impious to say that, when something extraordinary
happens in favor of someone, such a favor does not come with
the approval and plan of God. Accordingly, it is pious to admit
the contrary. The Roman Empire was helped to its fulfillment
by divine intervention and aid; therefore, it was willed by God
and consequently existed and still exists by right.

[12] XII. 936. "You have conquered and now the Ausonians see me with
upturned palms; Lavinia is your wife."
[13] St. Thomas Aquinas *Summa contra gentiles* III. 101.

Now, that God used miracles for achieving the Roman Empire is attested by famous authors. Livy tells us in the first part of his work that when Numa Pompilius, the second king of the Romans, was officiating at the pagan sacrifices, a shield fell from heaven on God's chosen city. Lucan, in the ninth book of his *Pharsalia*, refers to this miracle when he is describing the incredible power of the south wind that blows over Libya; he says—

> Sic illa profecto
> sacrifico cecidere Nume, que lecta iuventus
> patricia cervice movet: spoliaverat auster
> aut boreas populos ancilia nostra ferentes.[14]

And when the Gauls, who had already captured the rest of the city, tried by stealth to scale the Capitoline Hill, which was all that remained to complete the destruction of the Roman name, it was a goose, till then unnoticed, that raised a cry and warned the Capitoline guards of the approach of the Gauls. Livy and many other great writers agree in their accounts of this event. And the Poet in his eighth book, where he describes Aeneas' shield, also recalls this event in the following verses—

> In summo custos Tarpeie Manlius arcis
> stabat pro templo et Capitolia celsa tenebat,
> Romuleoque recens horrebat regia culmo.
> Atque hic auratis volitans argenteus anser
> porticibus Gallos in limine adesse canebat.[15]

And Livy also relates in his book on the Punic Wars, where he tells of other exploits, how the Roman nobles were being hard pressed by Hannibal, so that it seemed as if the imminent as-

---

[14] IX. 477ff. "Thus there descended on Numa while he was performing the sacrifice the shield which is carried by the chosen patrician youth: the south wind or the north had robbed these peoples who carried our shields."

[15] VIII. 652ff. "Above all stood Manlius, the guard of the Tarpeian fortress, holding watch before the temple over the Capitoline; Romulus' palace was there all new with its fresh thatch. And there, fluttering among the gilded porticoes, was the goose, wrought in silver, which gave warning that the Gauls were at the very threshold."

sault on the city by the Carthaginians would be the end of
Rome, and how a hailstorm broke over them so savagely that
the victors were unable to follow up their victory. And was not
Cloelia's escape miraculous? She was held captive by Porsena
during the siege, but, though a woman, she broke away from
her chains through divine aid and was enabled to swim the
Tiber. Is it any wonder that almost all the Roman historians
sing her praises?

It was fitting that He who foresees everything beautifully
ordered in a single frame should work in this manner; that He,
become visible in miracle, should make the invisible manifest,
and being Himself invisible, should show Himself through
these visible events.

5

Roman rule was for the common good.

Whoever is mindful of the good of the commonwealth is *ipso
facto* mindful of the purpose of right. The truth of this proposition is proved as follows: The definition of right given in the
Digests of Law, namely, "Right is a real and personal bond between man and man whose preservation preserves society and
whose corruption corrupts society," is not a definition of the essence of right, but a description of its utility. If this definition
is nevertheless a good account of what right is in practice and
what it comprises, and if the purpose of any society is the common good of its members, the purpose of right must be to promote the common good, and anything that fails to promote it
cannot possibly be right. Cicero says this very well at the beginning of his *Rhetoric*: "Laws should always be so interpreted as
to promote the good of the commonwealth." For if laws are not
useful to those who are governed by them, they are laws only in
name, not in fact. Laws should bind men together for their
mutual benefit, as Seneca said very truly in his book *On the
Four Virtues*: "Law is the bond of human society." Hence it is
clear that to be mindful of the good of the commonwealth is to
be mindful of the purpose of right. Now if the Romans actually

pursued the good of the commonwealth, it is true to say that they were faithful to the right. That the Roman people did pursue this good when they made the whole earth subject to them is proved by their deeds, for putting aside all greed as always incompatible with the commonwealth, and seeking universal peace with liberty, this holy, pious, and glorious people seemed to neglect its own interests in order to promote the public interest for the salvation of mankind. Hence it is truly said: "The Roman Empire springs from the fountain of piety." But since it is impossible to examine the intentions of a conscious agent directly, but only through external signs, and since, as I said, we must be guided by the nature of our subject, we shall give enough evidence for this contention if we enumerate indubitable signs of the motives of the Romans, taking them both collectively and individually.

Concerning the Roman organized public bodies, which were a kind of bond by which men were tied to the commonwealth, it suffices to mention only the authority of Cicero, in *De officiis* II: "As long as the power [*imperium*] of the commonwealth was based on benefits, not on injuries, wars were waged either on behalf of allies or to maintain its power, and the consequences of these wars were either mild or necessary; the senate was a haven of refuge for kings, peoples, and nations. Our magistrates and commanders [*imperatores*] were most eager to be praised for defending the provinces and allies in equity and fidelity. And therefore the rule of Rome could be called a paternal care of the world rather than a world empire!" This from Cicero!

Now taking Romans individually, I shall be brief. Who can refrain from calling them mindful of the common good when by sweat, by poverty, in exile, in loss of children, limbs, and even in the sacrifice of their very lives, they sought to promote the public weal? Did not Cincinnatus leave us a revered example of voluntarily resigning his public office when he had accomplished his mission? Livy tells the story of how he was taken from his plow and made dictator, and of how, after he had won his victory and celebrated his triumph, he returned to his plowing and to a life of sweaty toil behind his oxen. It was in his praise and in memory of his beneficence that Cicero wrote, in connection with his argument against Epicurus in *De fine bonorum,* "Thus our ancestors took a man like Cincinnatus from the plow and made him dictator." [16] And did not Fabricius give us a fine example of how to resist greed? He was a poor man, but in loyalty to the public weal he rejected the large sum of gold that was offered him, and in rejecting it spoke words of derision which were a fitting expression of his scorn of wealth. His memory is celebrated also by our Poet in his sixth book with the verse—

> *parvoque potentem*
> *Fabricium.*[17]

And was not Camillus a memorable example for us of how to put the laws above our own advantage? According to Livy, he had been condemned to exile and after he had freed his country from bondage and had restored her spoils to Rome and was being acclaimed by the whole people, he departed from the sacred city and refused to return until his return had been legalized by an act of the Senate. The Poet in his sixth book praises this magnanimous character by calling him

> *referentem signa Camillum.*[18]

And did not the first Brutus give us our lesson in subordinating our own children and all other cherished things to our country's liberty? Livy tells how when he was consul he had to condemn his own sons to death for conspiring with the enemy. Our Poet in his sixth book for Brutus' renown adds the verses—

> *natosque pater nova bella moventes*
> *ad penam pulcra pro libertate vocavit.*[19]

Are we not persuaded by Mucius of his boundless devotion to his country? He tried to kill Porsena when he had a chance

[16] *De finibus* II. 4.
[17] *Aeneid* VI. 843, "Fabricius, powerful in poverty."
[18] *Ibid.,* VI. 825, "Camillus returning the insignia."
[19] *Ibid.,* VI. 820, "A father who, when he discovers his children plotting fresh wars, condemns them for fair freedom's sake."

to do so, and when his attempt failed, he watched his hand, that had failed him, being burned as if it were an enemy being tortured. Livy expresses his admiration for the man about whom he tells this story.

Then there are those most venerated martyrs, the Decii, who dedicated their lives to death for the sake of the public good, whom Livy glorifies not as much as they deserve but as much as he can. Also, the unspeakable sacrifice of Marcus Cato, the strictest champion of true liberty. The Decii, for the good of their country, did not shrink from the horrors of the shadows of death; whereas Marcus Cato, to kindle the love of liberty in the world, showed how highly he valued liberty by freely preferring to depart from life rather than to remain living as a slave. The great names of these martyrs are exalted by the praises of Cicero, who speaks of them as follows in his books *De fine bonorum:* "Publius Decius, the first of his family to be consul, in sacrificing his life by driving his horse full speed into the midst of the Latins' spears, was he calculating what would give him the most pleasure and where and when he might get it, or, realizing that he would soon have to die, did he not seek the best death with more ardor than Epicurus would have thought it possible to seek pleasure? Had this his act not been praiseworthy, it would not have been imitated by his son, consul for the fourth time; nor would his son's son, also a consul, have followed the family tradition and offered his life in turn to the public, when he fell waging war against Pyrrhus." [20] And in his *De officiis* Cicero said of Cato: "The case of Marcus Cato was somewhat different from those who went to Africa and submitted to Caesar, for if they had killed themselves, the act might have been interpreted as a consequence of their more carefree lives and easier manners, whereas Cato's nature was extremely grave, and this gravity had been consistently displayed in his character, for he always kept before him his resolve that it is better to die than to bow to a tyrant." [21]

Two things have now been established: first, that all who

[20] *De finibus* II. 19.
[21] I. 112.

seek the good of the commonwealth seek the goal of right; and secondly, that the Roman people sought the goal of right in subjecting the world. Now we must prove that all who seek the goal of right do right. We have proved above that the Roman people sought the goal of right in subjecting the world. Now we must prove that when the Roman people subjected the world it did right, and that consequently it had a right to assume imperial dignity. This conclusion follows only if, as I said, we can prove that all who seek the goal of right do right. The first evidence to be noticed is that whatever exists, exists for some purpose, else it would be useless, which is impossible, as we showed earlier. And as everything has its own end, so every end has its own thing whose end it is. Hence two things, if they are really two, cannot aim at the same end; for then the untenable proposition would follow that one of them exists in vain. Now since we have already proved that the goal or end of right exists, we must admit the existence of right, since the goal is the specific and exclusive effect of right. And since in any causal sequence the antecedent implies the consequence (as man implies animal), and this is true both in affirmations and negations, it is impossible to seek the end of right without right, for end and means are related as consequence and antecedent. So, for example, it is impossible to attain a state of good health except by health. This makes it very clear that to seek the goal of right implies to seek it rightly.

It is no valid objection to this argument to quote the Philosopher's discussion of "good advice" [in the *Ethics*], where he says, "A true conclusion may be reached even by an invalid syllogism, though it is not reached truly, since the middle term must be ambiguous." For when a true conclusion is said to be drawn from false premises, it is not truly drawn as a conclusion, the truth being in the statement of the proposition, not in its being the conclusion of an argument. For a true conclusion never follows from false premises, though true words may be derived from words which are false. So too in matters of action. If a thief uses stolen goods to give alms to a pauper, he cannot be said truly to be giving alms; his act is rather one which would have been giving alms had he given what belonged to him. Similarly in the case of the goal of right. For if the goal of right, that is, the common good, were achieved unjustly, it would be the goal of right only in so far as it happens to be the common good, that is, in the same sense that the offering of ill-gotten goods can be alms. Thus the objection to our proposition does not hold if we keep in mind the existence of the goal of right and not its mere appearance. So our proof is valid.

6

The Roman capacity to rule proves that its rule was a natural order.

The order of nature is preserved *de jure*. For man's own provision for himself can not exceed natural providence, otherwise the effect would be better than the cause, which is impossible. We notice, for example, that the public administrator who organizes a body of officials must take into account not only the duties of each member in the body with respect to the others, but also the ability of each to perform his particular duty, which implies taking into account the limitations of responsibility both of the body of officials as a whole and of each member, for responsibility or right cannot exceed ability to perform. So nature is similarly prudent in its ordinations. Hence it is clear that nature orders things according to their powers, and this fundamental principle of right is built into the nature of things. It follows from this that the order of nature cannot be preserved without right action, for this order is inseparably linked with the foundations of right. Therefore the [natural] order is necessarily preserved *de jure*.

The Roman people was ordained by nature for rule. The proof is as follows: an artist would be imperfect who cared only for a final form and neglected the means of creating it; but nature is not imperfect, since it is the work of divine intelligence;

therefore nature intends whatever means are needed to arrive at its final intention. Now since mankind has a goal, and since nature must use means to achieve its universal goal, it is a necessary consequence that nature itself promotes man's goal. The Philosopher argues this thesis well in the second book of his *Physics,* where he maintains that nature always acts toward an end. Now since nature cannot achieve its end through one man alone, for its many works require many men, it must create many men ordained for diverse functions. For this multiplicity there needs must be, in addition to the influence from above, the various powers and aptitudes found here below. We can therefore observe how not only individual men but whole peoples are born, some fit to rule, others fit to be ruled and to serve. The Philosopher makes this observation in his book on *Politics;* and, as he says, it is not only expedient that those who are born to be ruled should be governed by others, but it is just, even when they must be forced into subjection.

In view of these facts there is no doubt that nature has ordained a place and nation in the world for universal rule, otherwise nature would be defective, which is impossible. As to what place and which nation was so ordained, the above reasons and those still to follow show that Rome was chosen, its citizens or people. This is suggested very subtly by our Poet in his sixth book, where Anchises is represented as making the following prophecy to Aeneas, father of the Romans—

> *Excudent alii spirantia mollius era,*
> *credo equidem; vivos ducent de marmore vultus;*
> *orabunt causas melius celique meatus*
> *describent radio et surgentia sidera dicent:*
> *tu regere imperio populos, Romane, memento.*
> *Hee tibi erunt artes, pacique imponere morem,*
> *parcere subiectis et debellare superbos.*[22]

22 VI. 847ff. "There shall be others, I know well, who more skillfully carve breathing beings from bronze and make lifelike faces of marble; others shall better plead cases and describe mathematically the heavenly movements, calculate the rising of the stars: Remember, Roman, that you are to govern peoples. These are your arts. You are to impose the ways of peace, sparing those who submit and being inexorable to the proud."

And in the fourth book he subtly mentions the Romans' location in the passage where Jove says to Mercury about Aeneas—

> *Non illum nobis genitrix pulcerrima talem*
> *promisit Graiumque ideo bis vindicat armis;*
> *sed fore qui gravidam imperiis belloque frementem*
> *Ytaliam regeret.*[23]

For all these reasons there is sufficient evidence that the Roman people was by nature ordained to rule: therefore, the Roman people in subjugating the world acquired its world power by right.

7

Kinds of divine judgment and revelation.

In order to arrive at the truth we are seeking, we must understand that the divine judgment in human affairs is sometimes revealed, sometimes hidden. It can be revealed in two ways: to reason and to faith. For certain judgments of God can be arrived at by human reason standing on its own legs—for example, the judgment that a man should give himself for the sake of his country. For if a part should give itself for the sake of the whole, and a man is a part of some community (as the Philosopher says in his *Politics*), a man should give himself for the sake of his country, as a lesser for a greater good; as the Philosopher puts it in the *Nicomachean Ethics*, "It is enjoyable to be of service to a single person, but better and more godlike to serve a people or a community." Now this is a judgment of God; were it not so, man's right reason would not serve nature's purpose, which is impossible.

There are other judgments of God to which human reason by its own resources can not attain, but to which it can be raised with the help of faith in what is told us in Holy Scripture. For instance, that none, however perfect in moral and intellectual virtues, in character and in deed, can be saved without faith,

---

[23] IV. 227ff. "Not for this did Venus, beautiful mother, promise him to us and twice save him from Grecian arms, but rather that he should rule Italy, a land heavy with empires and groaning with war."

though he never even heard of Christ; for to human reason alone this cannot appear just, but when aided by faith it may appear so. For in the letter to the Hebrews it is written, "Without faith it is impossible to please God"; and in Leviticus, "Any man of the house of Israel who shall slay an ox or a sheep or a goat in the camp or outside the camp, and shall not bring it as an oblation to the Lord at the door of the tabernacle, shall be guilty of blood." The door of the tabernacle is a figurative expression for Christ, who is the door of our eternal dwelling, as the Gospels say. The slaying of animals is a figurative expression for human deeds in general.

A hidden judgment of God is one which human reason cannot grasp either by natural law or by scriptural law, but only by some special grace. This may happen in various ways, which are all instances either of simple revelation or of revelation through ordeal. Simple revelations are of two kinds: spontaneous acts of God or answers to prayer. Spontaneous acts of God are of two kinds: either explicit (as the revelation against Saul to Samuel), or by sign (as the signs given to Pharaoh of Israel's deliverance). Answers to prayer are defined by the writer of II Chronicles: "When we know not what we should do, this only have we left, to turn our eyes to thee." Revelation through ordeals is of two kinds: by lot or by contest, for a contest is a kind of testing. By lot God's judgment is occasionally revealed, as when Matthew was substituted.[24] Contests for deciding God's judgment are of two kinds: either combats of men (as duels between champions) or competitions of men (when several rivals strive to win a set goal), as in the races of athletes. The first of these kinds of contest was symbolized in the Gentile tradition by the duel between Hercules and Antaeus, described by Lucan in the fourth book of his *Pharsalia* and by Ovid in the ninth book of *De rerum transmutatione;* the second kind is symbolized by the contest between Atlanta and Hippomenes in the tenth book of *De rerum transmutatione.*

It is important to note the difference between these two kinds

24 Acts 1:26.

of contest: in combat the contenders may, without doing wrong, take any advantage they can, whereas in competitions the rules of fair play may not be violated, for athletes may not foul, even though our Poet, in his fifth book, seems to be of a contrary opinion when he has the prize go to Euryalus. Therefore Cicero is better, in the third book of *De officiis,* where, following the judgment of Chrysippus, he repudiates this view and says, "Chrysippus as usual knew what he was saying when he declared that 'anyone who races in the stadium should try to win and should use all means possible, except that he may not foul his opponent.'"

Now with these distinctions in mind we can develop two arguments in behalf of our thesis: one based on athletic competitions, the other on combats between champions. To these we now turn.

8

It was by divine will that the Romans prevailed in the athletic contest for world-rule.

The people which won over others in the athletic contest for world-power won by divine judgment. For God cares more about the outcome of a universal contest than of a special contest, and if in these special contests the athletes may be supposed to win by divine judgment (according to the proverb: "To whom God grants victory let Peter add a blessing"), there can be no doubt that God's judgment is followed in the outcome of athletes contending for world-rule. The Roman people won the prize of world-rule in athletic contest. To make this clear we must review the various contenders and consider the prize or goal. The prize or goal was dominion over all mortals; for this is what is meant by imperial power. But no one ever attained this goal except the Roman people; this people was not only the first but the only one ever to arrive at the finish of the race, as we shall now show. The first mortal to try for this prize was Ninus, King of Assyria. He tried, with the help of his queen, Semiramis, as Orosius tells the story, for ninety years and more to obtain by force of arms dominion over the whole world, and he did succeed in subjugating all Asia; but he never reached the extreme western regions. Ovid recalls both of these rulers in his fourth book, where Piramus says—

> *Coctilibus muris cinxisse Semiramis urbem*

and further on—

> *Conveniant ad busta Nini lateantque sub umbra.*[25]

The second to aspire to this prize was Vesoges [Rameses II], King of Egypt, who, though he conquered southern and northern Asia, according to Orosius, never controlled as much as half of the world, for the Scythians turned him from his ambitious attempt before he had covered half the course. Then Cyrus, King of Persia, tried it; after he had destroyed Babylon and annexed the Babylonian Empire, but even before he reached the West, he lost both his life and his plan at the hands of Tamiris, Queen of the Scythians. Then Xerxes, Darius' son and Persian King, made an invasion with so much power and so many people as to enable him to bridge the strait between Sestos and Abydos which separates Asia from Europe. Lucan makes mention of this wonderful accomplishment when he writes in his second book of the *Pharsalia*—

> *Talis fama canit tumidum super equora Xerxem construxisse viam.*[26]

Nevertheless he failed miserably in his undertaking and could not gain the prize. Then followed Alexander, King of Macedonia, who came closest to winning the palm of universal rule when he sent ambassadors to the Romans demanding their submission; but even before their reply reached him, he perished in Egypt, during mid-career. Livy narrates this event;

[25] *Metamorphoses*, IV. 58 and 88.
　　　"Semiramis encircled the city with brick walls...
　　They shall gather at Ninus' tomb and hide in the shade."
[26] II. 672ff. "The story is told of how proud Xerxes built a way across the waters."

and Lucan in his eighth book, where he inveighs against
Ptolemy, King of Egypt, refers to Alexander's being buried in
that country—

> *Ultima Lagee stirpis perituraque proles*
> *degener, inceste sceptris cessure sorori,*
> *cum tibi sacrati Macedo servetur in antro.*[27]

"Oh, the depth of the riches of the wisdom and knowledge
of God." Who is there who is not silenced by Thee? For Thou
didst certainly remove Alexander from the race when he com-
peted with Rome, so that his insolence might reach no further.

But Rome! Many are the witnesses to her carrying off the
palm of victory in this race. Thus our Poet says in his first
book—

> *Certe, hinc Romanos olim volventibus annis*
> *hinc fore ductores, revocato a sanguine Teucri*
> *qui mare, qui terras omni ditione tenerent.*[28]

And Lucan in his first book—

> *Dividitur ferro regnum populique potentis*
> *que mare, que terras, que totum possidet orbem*
> *non cepit fortuna duos.*[29]

And Boethius in his second book, where he speaks of the Roman Emperor, says—

> *Hic tamen sceptro populus regebat,*
> *quos videt condens radios sub undas*
> *Phebus extremo veniens ab ortu,*
> *quos premunt septem gelidi triones,*
> *quos nothus sicco violentus estu*
> *torret, ardentes recoquens arenas.*[30]

[27] *Pharsalia* VIII. 692ff. "And you, the last, degenerate member of
Lagus' tribe, shall perish, and your scepter shall pass to your incestuous
sister, while near you will rest the Macedonian in his sacred cave."

[28] *Aeneid* I. 234ff. "The revolving years shall surely raise to the Romans
leaders, sprung from renewed Teucrian blood, who shall hold sway over
the lands and the sea."

[29] *Pharsalia* I. 109ff. "Steel has divided the empire of that powerful
people who held the sea and the lands of the whole earth; Fortune could
allow no two such peoples."

[30] *De consolatione philosophiae* II. "With his scepter he ruled the

The same testimony comes to us from Christ's Evangelist,
Luke, who always speaks the truth and who writes the words:
"An edict went forth from Caesar Augustus that a census be
taken in the whole world"; from these words it follows that we
can plainly know that the Romans then had the authority to
rule the whole world.

These considerations prove that it was in a real athletic contest that the Roman people won against others, that it therefore
won as a result of divine judgment, and that it had a right to
its victory.

9

Rome won world-rule by ordeal, and hence by right.

But what is won in [nonathletic] combat, may also be won
de jure. For when human judgment is lacking either because it
is shrouded in the darkness of ignorance or because there is no
judge to preside, it becomes necessary, lest justice be forfeited,
to have recourse to someone who so loves the demands of justice that he will pay the price with his blood and life. Hence the
psalm, "Just is the Lord, and deeds of justice hath he loved."
This takes place when, with the free consent of the parties concerned, not in hatred but for love of justice, the divine judgment is sought by gathering the powers of mind and body in a
mutual test of strength. Such a clash is usually called a duel,
because it first took the form of letting two combatants fight.
But we must heed the warning that, as in warlike disputes, all
possible means of settling the dispute by discussion must first be
tried, and that battle is only a last resort. On this subject Cicero
in *De officiis* and Vegetius in *Re militari* agree. And as in
medicine all other remedies are tried before steel and fire,
which are a last resort, so in disputes all possible other ways of

---

peoples whom Phoebus sees where his car dips into the waves and where
it rises again out of the far East, where the frozen North weighs on them,
and where the violent south wind burns them with its hot breath and
bakes the burning sands."

getting judgment must be exhausted before we finally resort to this remedy, as if we were forced to it by the need for justice.

A combat, then, has two formal characteristics: first, as we have just said [it is a last resort], and second, as we said above, it is waged neither out of hatred nor love, for it is only out of a zeal for justice and by common consent that contenders or duelists should enter the field. On this subject Cicero has spoken well: "When wars are waged for the crown of empire they should be waged less bitterly." Now, if the formal requisites of a combat are adhered to (otherwise a struggle is not a combat), and men are gathered in need of justice and by common consent in order to show their zeal for justice, are they not gathered in the name of God? And if so, is not God in their midst, as he has promised us in the Gospel? And if God be present, is it not impious to believe that justice may not be done by one who loves it so much (as above explained)? And if justice can not be suppressed in such combat, are not the fruits of the combat acquired *de jure*? This is a truth acknowledged even by the Gentiles before the trumpet of the Gospel had sounded, for they sought a judgment in the fortunes of combat. So, for example, the illustrious Pyrrhus, worthy descendant of the Aeacidae in blood and conduct, made an excellent reply when the Roman legates were sent to him to negotiate the release of captives. "I do not seek gold," he said, "and you need not offer me a price. We are not merchants of war, but wagers of war. By sword, not gold, we shall settle who shall live. Let us try through valor to learn whom of us Hera wishes to rule. Those whom fortune spares by their valor may certainly have their freedom from me. I give them to you to lead away." In these words Pyrrhus invokes Hera, or Fortune, whereas we may more properly and justly call such judgment that of divine providence.

In view of these considerations, let fighters beware before they agree to champion a cause for money; they thus transform an ordeal into a market where blood and injustice are bought and sold. And let them not suppose that it is God who sits in judgment over them, but rather that same ancient enemy who incited them to strife. Let them always have Pyrrhus before their eyes and his reply over the doorway to the arena, if they wish to be champions and not mere traffickers in blood and injustice; for he, as I have said, despised gold when it came to a contest for world-rule. If the usual objections are made to this truth because champions are of unequal strength, the answer is found in the victory of David over Goliath. And if the Gentiles wish a different illustration, let them consider the victory of Hercules over Antaeus. For it is foolish to imagine that the powers that God wields are less than those of a prize fighter.

It is now sufficiently clear how it is possible that what is acquired by combat may also be acquired by right.

10

By single combat the Romans rightly won "the crown of righteousness."

It was by single combat that the Romans achieved their world-rule. This can be proved by reliable witnesses who bear evidence for this and who also show that from the earliest days of the Roman Empire decisions were reached by means of duels. At the very outset, when a dispute arose between Aeneas and Turnus, the king of the Rutuli, concerning the estate to be assigned to father Aeneas, both kings agreed finally to seek the divine pleasure by waging a single combat. The story is told in the last book of the Aeneid. In this combat, according to our Poet's verses, the clemency of Aeneas, the victor, was so great that he would have spared the life of the vanquished and offered him peace, had he not happened to notice the belt which Turnus had taken from Pallas after killing him. And when in the course of time two branches of the Trojan family grew up in Italy, the Romans and the Albans, who fought for a long time for the right to the symbol of the eagle, to the Trojan household gods, and to the dignity of supremacy, both peoples, in order to know the final verdict, agreed that the three Horatii brothers on the one side and the three Curiatii brothers on the other should wage a public combat before the two kings and their peoples. When all three Alban champions had been killed and two of the Romans, the palm of victory was awarded to the Romans under King Hostilius. Livy describes this incident in detail in the first part of his *History,* and Orosius' account agrees. Further on Livy tells of other combats with the neighboring Sabines and Samnites, in which the rights of war and the rules of single combat were scrupulously observed even when the champions were composed of large groups. Hence, as in the case of the Samnites, a slight turn of events might have caused Fortune to repent, so to say, in shaping destiny. Lucan uses this as an illustration in his second book, as follows:

> *Aut Collina tulit stratas quot porta catervas*
> *tunc cum pene caput mundi rerumque potestas*
> *mutavit translata locum, Romanaque Samnis*
> *ultra Caudinas speravit vulnera furcas.*[31]

Hardly had these disputes among the Italian peoples been settled, when Rome, struggling to obtain the divine favor in many military combats, won the glory of world-rule from the Greeks as well as from the Carthaginians; as if Fabricius were champion of the Romans and Pyrrhus of the Greeks, or Scipio champion of the Italians and Hannibal of the Africans. The Africans yielded to the Italians, as Livy and other Roman historians all testify.

Now who can be so dull-witted as not to see that by ordeal the glorious people won for itself by right the crown of the whole world? Well might a Roman have said what the Apostle said to Timothy, "There is laid up for me a crown of righteousness"—laid up, that is, in the eternal providence of God. Let the presumptuous lawyers now see how far they are below the lookout tower of human reason, whence these principles can be viewed. Let them be silent and mind their own business of interpreting the meaning and decisions of the law.

---

[31] *Pharsalia* II. 135ff. "And how many corpses the Colline gate had to hold at a critical moment when the seat of world-government and power almost shifted from one place to another, and the Samnite expected to see a Rome more wounded than by the Caudine Forks."

We have now shown that the Roman people acquired empire by ordeal and hence by right, which is the proposition to be proved in this book. So far our proof has rested on rational principles chiefly; now we shall prove our proposition by the principles of Christian faith.

11

That Rome enjoyed divine authority is shown by Christ's birth.

For they have been the first to rage and meditate vain things against Roman authority who call themselves the defenders of the Christian faith. Not only have they no pity for Christ's poor, whom they defraud with their ecclesiastical revenues, but they plunder daily the patrimony of the Church itself, and the Church is impoverished. While they simulate justice, they exclude those who would do justice. Such impoverishment does not escape divine judgment, for the ecclesiastical funds are neither used for the relief of the poor, to whom they rightly belong, nor are they accepted gratefully as gifts from the Emperor who grants them. Let them return whence they came! They came well, they return ill. For they were well given and badly invested. But why should such shepherds care? What is the wasting away of the Church's substance to them, so long as their own kin flourish! But perhaps we had better return to our subject, and in devout silence await our Saviour's help!

So I maintain that if the Roman Empire did not exist *de jure,* Christ's birth implies an injustice. The consequence is false, therefore the contradictory of the antecedent is true, for of contradictory propositions one is true and the other false. It is needless to prove the falsity of the consequent to the faithful, for anyone who is faithful will admit the falsity of that proposition. If not, he is unfaithful. And if he is not of the faith, he will have no interest in this proof. The argument runs as follows: Anyone who voluntarily submits to an edict proves by his deed that he regards the edict as just, for since deeds are more powerful arguments than words (as the Philosopher says toward the end of the *Nicomachean Ethics*), his act was a better evidence than if he had approved it in words. But Christ, as his scribe Luke testifies, willed to be born of the Virgin Mary under an edict of Roman authority in order that he, the Son of God made man, might register in that extraordinary register of mankind as a man; thus he recognized its legality. Of course, a more devout way of putting this would be that by a divine decision the edict was given by Caesar, in order that he who had been awaited for ages to appear in the society of mortals might associate himself with mortals. Therefore Christ signified by his coming that the edict given by Augustus, under the authority of the Romans, was just. And since the issuing of an edict justly implies the jurisdiction of its author, Christ recognized Caesar's jurisdiction, for a just edict must be issued *de jure*. We might note that this argument for refuting the above consequence is valid in any form, but it seems to have more force when put in the second [negative] figure of the syllogism, instead of, as above, in the first figure, thus—

> All unjust deeds give false evidence
> Christ did not give false evidence
> Christ did not give evidence of anything unjust,

whereas in the first figure it was—

> All unjust deeds give false evidence
> Christ did something unjust
> Christ gave false evidence.

12

Rome's divine authority is shown also by Christ's submission to Roman law.

Had the Roman Empire not existed *de jure*, Adam's sins would not have been punished in Christ. But this is false. Therefore the contradictory of the antecedent is true. The falsity of the consequent is clear from the following considerations: By Adam's sin we are all sinners, as the Apostle says: "As

by one man sin entered into this world, and by sin death; and
so death passed upon all men, because all have sinned." [32]
Now, if satisfaction for this sin had not been made by the death
of Christ, we would still be sons of wrath by nature, that is, by
our depraved nature. But this is not the case, for the Apostle,
writing to the Ephesians, says of the Father that "He hath pre-
destinated us unto the adoption of children through Jesus
Christ unto himself, according to the purpose of his will: Unto
the praise of the glory of his grace, in which he hath graced us
in his beloved son. In whom we have redemption through his
blood, the remission of sins, according to the riches of his glory,
which hath superabounded in us." [33] And Christ himself, as he
endured the punishment, said, according to John, "It is consummated." If consummated, nothing more needs to be done.

To understand the meaning of this, we must know that punishment is not merely the infliction of an injury, but an injury
inflicted by someone who has penal jurisdiction. Hence a penalty inflicted by an unqualified judge is not punishment, but
rather an injury. Thus a man said to Moses, "Who ordained
thee a judge over us?" So, if Christ had not suffered under an
authoritative judge, his penalty would not have been a punishment. Now that judge could not have been authorized unless
he had authority over all mankind, since Christ was bearing in
his flesh all "our sorrows," as the Prophet says, and all in him
were punished. And Tiberius Caesar, whom Pilate represented,
could not have had jurisdiction over the whole of mankind
had not the Roman Empire existed *de jure*. This is why Herod
unwittingly, like Caiphas when he spoke truly about the heavenly decree, sent Christ back to Pilate to be judged, as Luke
tells in his Gospel. For Herod did not rule under Tiberius as
under the eagle, the sign of the Senate's authority, but as a
king assigned by him to govern a special province, and he ruled
under the seal of that province.

Wherefore let them cease reproaching the Roman Empire
who call themselves sons of the Church, when they see that

[32] Romans 5:12.
[33] Eph. 1:5-8.

Christ, the Bridegroom of the Church, confirmed Roman authority at both ends of his militant career. And now I believe it is clear enough that the Roman people acquired by right its reign over the world. O happy people! O still glorious thou, Ausonia, had he [Constantine] who weakened thy power never been born or never been misled by his pious intentions!

BOOK THREE

THAT TEMPORAL WORLD-RULE CAME DIRECT FROM GOD AND NOT FROM THE PAPACY

1

The doctrine of this book is offensive to the Roman pontiff.

"He hath shut up the mouths of the lions, and they have not hurt me: forasmuch as before him justice hath been found in me." [1] At the beginning of this work we undertook to answer three questions in so far as their natures permitted answers. Of these, two have been sufficiently treated, I believe, in the foregoing books. Now it remains to treat the third, whose true solution may bring upon me a certain amount of indignation on the part of those whom the bare truth will cause to blush. But since Truth herself from her immutable throne bids us to do as Solomon did when he entered the forest of proverbs, to fix our eyes on her and scorn her impious detractors, and since the Philosopher and moral preceptor urges us to sacrifice even friendship for the sake of truth, I take courage from the above words of Daniel which declare that a divine power shields the champions of the truth, and, following Paul's advice, I put on the breastplate of faith; and with the heat of the coal snatched by a seraph from the heavenly altar, wherewith he touched the lips of Isaiah, I now enter the arena, and shall hurl out the impious liar in the sight of all the world. What should I fear? When the Spirit of the Father, coeternal with the Son, says through David's mouth: "The just shall be in everlasting remembrance: he shall not fear the evil hearing." [2]

1 Daniel 6:22.
2 Psalm 111:6-7.

52

The present question which we are about to examine divides two great luminaries, the Roman pontiff and the Roman prince. Does the authority of the Roman ruler, who, as we have shown in Book II, is the *de jure* ruler of the world, come directly from God or through some vicar or minister of God, I mean Peter's successor, who truly holds the keys to the kingdom of heaven?

2

Whatever does not come about naturally is not of divine will.

In raising this issue we must lay down, as we did in the previous books, some principle on whose strength our arguments for the true conclusion may rest. For there is no use in working without a pre-established principle, even when one is telling the truth, since all the middle terms of our argument are rooted entirely in a principle. Let this, then, be prefixed as an unassailable truth, that God does not will what is contrary to nature's intention. If this were not true, its contradictory would not be false, namely, "God is not unwilling when something goes contrary to nature's intention." And if this be not false, neither are its consequences, for when things are related by necessity, the consequent cannot be false unless the antecedent is.

Now there are necessarily two possible consequences of "not being unwilling," either "being willing" or "not willing at all," just as "not hating" implies either "loving" or "absence of loving," for "not loving" does not necessarily mean "hating"; and so "not to will" does not necessarily mean "to will not to . . . ." This is clear. Now if the above consequences are not false, then neither is it false that "God wills what he does not will," than which nothing could be more false.

Now, to prove that what I say is true, I maintain that God wills what nature intends, otherwise, for example, the heavens move in vain, which no one would maintain. If God should will an impediment to such an end, he would will that this end be impeded, otherwise his willing would be in vain. And since the purpose of an impediment is to prevent the existence of what

is impeded, it would follow that God (who, we said, wills nature's end) would will that a natural end should not exist.

If, on the other hand, God should not will an impediment to
such an end, in the sense that he has no will in this matter, we
may infer that his not willing meant merely that he did not
care whether the impediment existed or not. But anyone who is
indifferent to an impediment is indifferent to the end impeded,
and hence does not contain it in his will, and whatever is not
in his will he does not will. Hence, if a natural end can be impeded and really is impeded, it follows that God does not will
this natural end; and thus it would follow, as in the case of the
other [alternative interpretation of "not willing"], that God
wills what he does not will.

Therefore a proposition from whose contradictory such ab-
surdities follow must be most true.

3

*The authority of the Church does not rest on tradition, but
the authority of tradition on the authority of the Church.*

In entering upon this question we should be aware that the
discovery of the truth concerning the first of our questions was
more a matter of dispelling ignorance than of settling a dispute, whereas the second question was almost equally a matter
of ignorance and of dispute. There are many things about
which we are ignorant but which are not subjects of dispute:
the geometers do not know how to square the circle, but they
do not dispute the question; the theologians do not know how
many angels there are, but they do not debate the issue; the
Egyptians know nothing about the civilization of the Scythians,
but they do not argue about it. In the case of our third question, however, the chief cause of our ignorance of the truth is
our contention, whereas usually the chief cause of contention
is ignorance. For it always happens among men whose wills fly
ahead of their rational insight that in their bad temper they

put the light of reason behind them, and they proceed practically blinded by their tempers, but obstinately denying their blindness. The result is not only that error often reigns over an exclusive domain, but that many leave this domain [where they belong] and trespass on other encampments, where, lacking understanding, they are not understood; and they provoke some to anger, others to indignation, and still others to ridicule.

There are three kinds of men who most violently oppose the truth we are seeking. First, there is the supreme pontiff, Vicar of our Lord Jesus Christ and successor to Peter, to whom we owe what is due Peter but not all that is due Christ. In his zeal for the keys, perhaps, he, along with other shepherds of Christian flocks, and with certain laymen who, I believe, are also moved wholly by zeal for mother Church—they all deny the truth which I am about to show, not out of pride but perhaps, as I said, out of zeal.

Secondly, there are those whose light of reason has been extinguished by stubborn greed. Pretending to be the sons of the Church, they are children of the devil, and they dispute not only on this question, but in their hatred for the very name of the most holy Empire they impudently deny the very principles of our other questions as well as of this.

Then there is a third group, called Decretalists, who, being ignorant and unskilled in any theology or philosophy whatever, and resting their whole case on their decretals (which I, too, deem worthy of respect) denounce the Empire in the hope, I believe, that these decretals will prevail. At this I do not wonder, for I heard one of them say and even volubly insist that the Church's traditions are the foundation of the faith. May such a wicked idea be banished from the minds of mortals by the fact that before there were any ecclesiastical traditions there were those who believed in Christ, the Son of God, either as to come, or as present, or as having already suffered. No one in the world doubts that in this faith they had hope, and in their hope an ardent charity, and that in their zeal they were made coheirs with Christ. The whole group of Decretalists we can throw out of the present arena by showing that some scripture is prior to the Church, that some of it belongs to the Church, and that some of it is consequent to the Church.

Prior to the Church are the Old and New Testaments, given in eternity, as the Prophet says, when he represents the Church saying to her Bridegroom, "Draw me after thee." [3] With the Church came the great councils which should be revered, since no one doubts that Christ was present in them, for as he was about to ascend to heaven, he told his disciples, "Behold, I am with you all days, even to the consummation of the world," as Matthew bears witness.[4] With the Church are also the writings of its doctors, Augustine and the others, whom the Holy Spirit guided, as anyone would agree who has seen their fruits, and as those certainly would who have tasted them. But consequent to the Church came the traditions called "Decretals," which are also to be revered because they have apostolic authority, but which should undoubtedly be subordinated to the basic Scriptures. Christ himself reproached the priests for the contrary belief when they asked him, "Why do your disciples transgress the tradition of the elders?" (for they neglected the handwashing), and he answered (according to Matthew's testimony), "And why do ye transgress the commandment of God for the sake of your tradition?" This clearly assigns to tradition a subordinate rank. So, if the traditions come from the Church, as we have explained, and not the Church from the traditions, authority descends from the Church onto the traditions. Those who rely solely on the traditions, therefore, must be thrown out of the arena, as I said. For anyone who wishes to pursue our investigation must get down to the truth which flows from the sources of the Church's authority.

With this third group thrown out, we must now throw out those who go about in the Lord's flock decked out with crows' feathers, yet imagining themselves to be white sheep. These are the sons of impiety who, in pursuing their infamous course, prostitute their mother, drive out their brothers, and refuse to

[3] Song of Songs 1:13.
[4] Matthew 28:20.

submit to a judge. There is no point in bringing argument to bear on them, since their greed makes it impossible for them to see even first principles.

Thus there are left in our ring only those who out of zeal for mother Church are induced to ignore the very truth which we are seeking. It is against them that I now begin the contest of this book, in the spirit of reverence which a dutiful son owes to father and mother, to Christ and the Church, out of duty to his Shepherd and to all who profess the Christian religion.

4

The analogy of sun and moon is not applicable to temporal authority, as if it were reflected from the divine right of spiritual authority.

It is asserted by those against whom the remaining discussion is directed that the Empire's authority is subordinate to the Church's, as a workman is under the direction of an architect. They use several different arguments, based some of them on the Holy Scripture and some on the deeds of either popes or emperors from whose deeds they make certain theoretical inferences.

They say, in the first place, that, according to Genesis, God created two great luminaries, a greater and a lesser, one to govern the day and the other the night. This, they say, is an allegory for two types of power, spiritual and temporal. Then they argue that as the lesser luminary, the moon, has no light of its own except as it receives it from the sun, so temporal power has no authority except as it is derived from spiritual.

To overthrow this and other arguments of theirs, we should note that, as the Philosopher says in his treatise on *Fallacies,* the way to win an argument is to expose an error. Now since error can lie either in the substance or the form of an argument, there are two kinds of fallacies: assuming what is false or inferring incorrectly. The Philosopher objected to Parmenides and Melissus on both these grounds, saying, "They admit falsehoods and they don't know how to make syllogisms." Here I include under "false" also improbable opinions, for in questions of probable knowledge they have the force of falsehoods. If the fallacy is formal, the critic must destroy the conclusion by showing that the syllogistic structure has been violated. But if the fallacy is material, it is either a case of assuming what is wholly false or relatively false. If an assumption is wholly false, one of the premises must be denied; if it is relatively false, a distinction must be made.

With this procedure in mind, we can better criticize this and the following arguments if we call attention to two types of fallacious appeals to a mystic interpretation: either looking for it where it does not exist, or accepting a meaning which is improper. Regarding the first type, Augustine says in his *City of God,* "Not everything narrated is significant, for the insignificant must be narrated in order to bring out the significant. The plowshare alone turns the furrow, but the other parts of the plow are also needed." Concerning the second type, too, Augustine has something to say in his *Christian Doctrine,* when he is speaking about those who seek a meaning different from the author's intention and says that they make the same mistake that a traveler makes who leaves the road but finally in his digression arrives at the same point to which the road leads; and he adds, "Such a person should be warned that his bad habit of leaving the road may lead him onto crossroads and wrong roads." Then he gives the specific reason why this is a dangerous way of treating Holy Scripture, saying, "Faith will totter if the authority of the divine Scriptures vacillates." For my part I would say that if such mistakes arise from ignorance, we should carefully correct and pardon them, as we would a person who is afraid of lions in the clouds; but, if they are committed purposely, such interpreters should be treated not as ignoramuses but more as we would treat a tyrant who does not use public regulations for the common welfare but tries to twist their meaning for his own purposes. O greatest of crimes, to abuse the intention of the eternal Spirit, even if it happens in dreams! For the sin is not against Moses, or David, or Job, or Matthew, or Paul, but against the Holy Spirit, who speaks through them. For though there may be many writers of the divine word, there is but one who dictates it, namely, God, who was pleased to reveal himself to us by using many pens.

After these preliminary observations I can return to the criticism of the argument according to which the two luminaries signify two types of government, an argument which rests entirely on this analogy. There are two ways of showing that this interpretation of the passage in Genesis is inadmissible. First, since governments are not in the essence of human existence but in its circumstantial conditions or "accidents," God would have been guilty of creating backwards if he had first created types of government and then had created man, which would be absurd to attribute to God. For he made the two luminaries on the fourth day and man on the sixth, according to the text. Besides, since governments exist to guide men toward specific goals, as we shall show, there would have been no use for them if man had remained in the state of innocence in which he was created. For devices such as governments are remedies for the infirmity of sin. Since man was not only not a sinner on the fourth day but didn't exist at all, God would not have acted in accordance with his goodness if he had devised remedies on the fourth day. For it would be a silly physician who prepared a plaster to apply to the future abscess of an unknown person. It is therefore impossible to maintain that God created governments on the fourth day, and therefore Moses must have meant something different from what they imagine.

But this falsehood can also be destroyed by using the gentler method of exposing a material fallacy, and instead of calling the opponent an out-and-out liar, we can make a distinction which he overlooked. Thus I maintain that from the fact that the moon does not shine brightly unless it receives light from the sun, it does not follow that the moon itself depends on the sun. For one must keep in mind that the being of the moon is one thing, its power another, and its functioning a third. In its being the moon is in no way dependent on the sun, and not even in its power and functioning, strictly speaking, for its motion comes directly from the prime mover, some of whose rays shine on it. For it has a little light of its own, as we observe in eclipses, but in order to increase its power and efficacy it gets light from the sun, where it is plentiful. In like manner, I maintain, temporal power receives from spiritual power neither its being, nor its power or authority, nor even its functioning, strictly speaking, but what it receives is the light of grace, which God in heaven and the pope's blessing on earth cause to shine on it in order that it may work more effectively.

Lastly, there is a formal fallacy in their argument, for the predicate of the conclusion is not identical with that of the major premise, as it should be. Their argument runs thus: the moon receives light from the sun or spiritual power; the temporal power is the moon; therefore the temporal power receives its authority from the spiritual power. In the major premise it is light that the moon receives and in the conclusion it is authority, which are two quite different things, both as to their substance and their meaning, as I have explained.

5

The analogy of Levi and Judah is also invalid.

They also derive an argument from the Books of Moses, saying that from the loins of Jacob came the symbol of these two powers, namely, Levi and Judah, the first of whom was the father of the priesthood, and the other, of the temporal power. Hence, they reason as follows: the relation that obtained between Levi and Judah obtains also between Church and Empire; Levi was older in years than Judah, as the text records, therefore the Church precedes the Empire in authority. This can be refuted easily. For, since they say that Levi and Judah, sons of Jacob, prefigure the two types of power, I could simply deny their symbolism, and with equal reason. And when they say that "as Levi was the older, so is the Church's authority," I can point out that the predicate of the conclusion is not identical with the middle term; for "authority" and "age" are two

different things both in matter and in reason; hence there is
here a formal fallacy. Their argument goes: A precedes B in C;
D and E are related as A and B, therefore D precedes E in F.
But F and C are different. And if they continue to insist, saying that F follows from C, that is, that authority comes from
birth, being its logical antecedent, as animal antecedes man, I
say that is false. For there are many who are elders by birth,
who not only are not elders in authority but are even subject
to their juniors, as in the case of those bishops who are younger
than their elder-deacons. Thus the error of this argument is
clear: it takes as a causal relation what is not a causal relation.

6

Likewise, the analogy of Samuel and Saul.

From the text of the First Book of Kings they take the election and rejection of Saul, and say that Saul was both en-
throned as king by Samuel and then deposed by him, who
functioned as God's vicar, as the text makes clear. And on the
basis of this fact they reason that just as God gave Samuel the
authority to give and take temporal power and to transfer such
power, so he gives it still to his vicar, and that the head of the
universal church has the authority to give, take, and transfer
the scepter of temporal power; whence it would follow indubi-
tably that the imperial authority depends on the Church, as
they affirm.

To refute what they affirm about Samuel being God's vicar,
we must say that he acted not as God's vicar but as a nuncio or
legate sent on a special mission given him expressly by God,
which he then performed; this is clear because he said and did
only what God ordered him to say and do. Hence it is important to distinguish between a vicar and a nuncio or minister;
just as there is a difference between being a teacher and being
an interpreter. For a vicar has authority to legislate and to de-
cide, within the limits of his jurisdiction, in matters of which
his lord may be ignorant. But a nuncio can not do so as a mes-

senger; as a hammer acts only in virtue of the carpenter, so a messenger acts only in accord with the decision of him who has sent him. Hence it does not follow that a vicar can do what God ordered a special messenger to do. For God has done, still does, and will continue to do many things by angels which his vicar, as successor to Peter, may not do. Hence, they reason fallaciously from whole to part, thus: a man can hear and see, therefore an eye can hear and see. This does not hold, but negatively it would hold: thus, a man can not fly, therefore neither can his arm fly. Similarly, God can not by a messenger cause something that has happened not to have happened, to use an illustration of Agathon's; therefore, neither can God's vicar do so.

7

God's holding both temporal and spiritual power is not transferred to His vicar.

They also infer from the words of Matthew (2:11), who relates that the Magi offered to Christ both gold and incense, that he is lord of spiritual and temporal goods; whence they conclude that Christ was both lord and governor, and that he therefore possesses both kinds of authority. In reply, I admit the literal truth of what Matthew says, but deny what they infer from it. Their reasoning is as follows: God is lord of spiritual and temporal affairs; the supreme Pontiff is God's vicar; therefore, he is lord of spiritual and temporal affairs. Both premises are true, but the conclusion is based on four terms, which is syllogistically invalid. This is clear from the general principles of the syllogism. For "God" in the major premise is different from "vicar of God" in the predicate of the minor premise. And it is useless to insist that they are equivalent. For no vicar either of God or man is equivalent to the source of his authority; this is obvious. For we know that in natural processes Peter's successor is not a power equivalent to the divine authority; for he cannot make earth rise nor fire fall through the authority granted to him. Nor is it possible that

God committed all things to his care, such as power to create or to baptize, which God can not delegate. This is evident notwithstanding what the author of the *Sentences* says to the contrary in his fourth book. For we know that the vicar of a man is not his equivalent, being a vicar; for no one can give what is not his. Governmental authority is exercised by a government, but is not its own creation, for no government can authorize itself. It can receive or resign its authority, but cannot create another government, for such an act of creation is not a governmental act. If this is so, it is clear that no governor can create his vicar as a substitute, equivalent to him in all things. Hence this argument has no force.

8

Christ's conferring of the power of binding and loosing on Peter does not apply to temporal jurisdiction.

They also use the text in which Christ says to Peter, "And whatsoever thou shalt bind upon earth, it shall be bound also in heaven; and whatsoever thou shalt loose on earth, it shall be loosed also in heaven." [5] They admit that, both on the basis of Matthew and of John, Christ said the same to all the apostles. But they argue that by God's grant Peter's successors can bind or loose all things, and hence, they infer, they can loose the imperial laws and decrees, and bind the temporal power with their own laws and decrees; and from this power all the consequences follow that they claim.

I criticize this argument by distinguishing two uses of the major term of this syllogism. For their syllogism runs:

> Peter could loose or bind all things
> Peter's successor can do what Peter could
> therefore Peter's successor can loose or bind all things.

Hence they infer he can loose or bind the authority and decrees of the Empire. The minor I admit, but not the major

[5] Matthew 16:19.

without qualification. For I must explain that the universal word "all things," implied by "whatsoever," includes only "all things" relevant to the proposition in which it occurs. For, if I say "all animals run," "all" includes every animal; but if I say "all men run," "all" includes only men; and when I say "all grammarians," it is a still more restricted "all." So we must always look to see to what class of things "all" is applied in a given proposition; we can then tell readily how much is included in it when we know the nature and extent of the term to which it applies. Now, when the text says "whatever you bind," if this "whatever" is taken absolutely, then what they say is true; and the pope could do not only what they say, but he could loose a man's wife and could bind her to another, while her first husband is still living; which he cannot do. He could also absolve me from sin though I am not penitent; which God himself cannot do. Therefore it is clear "whatsoever" can not be taken absolutely but must be related to a particular class of things. What the class of things was to which the text refers in connection with Christ's grant of power is clear enough. For Christ said to Peter, "I will give thee the keys of the kingdom of heaven." That is, "I will make you the doorkeeper of the kingdom of heaven." Then he adds, "and whatsoever"; that is, "all which"; that is, "all which is connected with that office you may loose or bind." In this way we see that the logical context of the universal "whatsoever" is the power of the keys to the kingdom of heaven. In this sense the major premise is true, but evidently not when taken absolutely. And so I maintain that though Peter's successor may loose or bind in performing the duties of the office entrusted to Peter, it does not follow that he can therefore loose or bind imperial laws or decrees, as they maintain, unless it can be proved that this is related to the power of the keys; and it is the contrary of this which I shall prove [in chapter 14].

9

The "two swords" of temporal and spiritual power are not in the hands of the Church.

They also use the text in Luke where Peter says to Christ, "Lo, here are two swords," [6] and they claim that the two swords refer to the above-mentioned two types of government which, as Peter said, would be where he is, that is, with him. Whence they argue that the authority for both types of power resides in Peter's successor. Against this position we contend by denying that they interpret the meaning of the text correctly. Their claim that by the two swords Peter meant the two types of government must be denied flatly, both because such an interpretation would not have been a proper reply to what Christ meant to say, and because Peter, as usual, replied hastily to the obvious meaning.

That such a meaning would not have been an intelligible reply to what Christ said will become clearer if we examine what had been said before and the reason for saying it. We must remember that this conversation was on the day of the Last Supper, for Luke in an earlier verse begins: "And the day of the unleavened bread came, on which it was necessary that the paschal lamb should be killed." [7] At this supper Christ had intimated his approaching Passion, in which he would have to be separated from his disciples. We must also remember that during this conversation all twelve disciples were present. Accordingly Luke says, shortly after the quoted passage, "And when the hour had come, he sat down, and the twelve apostles with him." [8] Then, without interruption, he continues, "When I sent you without purse, and scrip, and shoes, did you want anything?" But they said: "Nothing." Then said he unto them: "But now he that hath a purse, let him take it, and likewise a scrip; and he that hath not, let him sell his coat, and buy a

[6] Luke 22:38.   [7] Luke 22:7.   [8] Luke 22:14.

sword." [9] Here Christ's meaning is clear enough; for he did
not say, "Buy two swords unless you already have them"; he
said, "Buy twelve," for to each he said, "Buy one, if you do
not have one," so that each would have a sword. He said all this
to warn them of the coming persecution and contempt, as if to
say: "As long as I was with you, you were received, but now
you will be put to flight; so in view of your coming needs you
should provide yourselves even with things which I have hither-
to prohibited." If, in his reply to these words, Peter meant
what they say he meant, he paid no attention to what Christ
meant, and Christ would have rebuked him as he often did
when Peter spoke carelessly. On this occasion, however, he did
not rebuke him but acquiesced, saying, "It is enough"; as if to
say, "I spoke in view of your need, but if you cannot each have
a sword, two will suffice."

That Peter was addressing his reply to the obvious meaning
is proved by his hasty and unconsidered presumptuousness, to
which he was impelled not only by the sincerity of his faith,
but also, as I believe, by a natural innocence and simplicity.
All the writers of Christ's Gospel testify to this presumptuousness of his. Matthew writes that once when Jesus asked the
disciples, "Whom do you say that I am?" [10] Peter was the first
to reply, "Thou art Christ, the Son of the living God." And he
further relates how, when Christ told his disciples that he
would have to go to Jerusalem and endure great suffering,
Peter interrupted and began to reproach him, saying, "Lord,
be it far from thee, this shall not be unto thee." [11] Christ then
turned to him and rebuked him with the words, "Go behind
me, Satan." Again he writes that on the mount of Transfigura-
tion when with the two sons of Zebedee he was face to face with
Christ, Moses, and Elias, he said: "Lord, it is good for us to be
here: if thou wilt, let us make here three tabernacles, one for
thee, and one for Moses, and one for Elias." [12] Again, he writes
that one night when the disciples were in a boat and Christ

9 Luke 22:35-36.   10 Matthew 16:15-16.
11 Matthew 16:22-23.   12 Matthew 17:4.

walked on the water, Peter said, "Lord, if It be thou, bid me come to thee upon the waters." [13] And he writes that when Christ forewarned his disciples that they would be scandalized by him, Peter replied, "Though all shall be scandalized in thee, I will never be scandalized," [14] and later, "Though I should die with thee, I will not deny thee." [15] Mark [14:29] tells this story, too. In addition, Luke writes that shortly before the saying about the two swords, Peter said to Christ, "Lord, I am ready to go with thee, both into prison and to death." [46] John relates that when Christ wanted to wash his feet, Peter said, "Lord, dost thou wash my feet?" and then, "Thou shalt never wash my feet." [17] He tells, as do all four evangelists, how Peter struck the minister's servant with his sword. And John says that when Peter saw the other disciple hesitating at the entrance to Christ's tomb, he walked straight in.

And after the resurrection when Jesus appeared on the seashore, he tells how Peter, as soon as he heard it was the Master, put on his cloak (for he was naked) and jumped from the boat into the sea. Lastly, he reports that when Peter saw John, he said to Jesus, "Lord, what shall this man do?" It is well to bring together all such incidents about our archimandrite in praise of his innocence, for they indicate clearly that when he spoke of the two swords he addressed himself to the obvious meaning of what Christ had said.

But, if after all this, these words of Christ and Peter must be interpreted symbolically, they should certainly not be interpreted as they are in papal theory, but should be referred to that sword of which Matthew writes: "Do not think that I came to send peace upon the earth: I came not to send peace, but the sword. For I came to set a man at variance against his father." [18] This was true, both in word and in deed, as Luke said to Theophilus, "What Jesus began to do and to teach." [19] This was the double sword which Christ recommended buying

[13] Matthew 14:28. [14] Matthew 26:33. [15] Matthew 26:35.
[16] Luke 22:33. [17] John 13:6, 8. [18] Matthew 10:34-35.
[19] Acts 1:1.

and which Peter declared to be already present. For both in
words and in deeds they were prepared to do what Christ said
he had come to do, as we have explained.

10

*Even if Constantine had donated imperial power to the
Church, he had no right to do so.*

Some use another argument, saying that the Emperor Constantine, at the time he was cleansed of his leprosy through the
intercession of Sylvester, who was then supreme Pontiff, donated
to the Church the Imperial seat, the City of Rome, together
with many other dignities of the Empire; from which they infer
that since that time no one can receive these dignities except
through the Church, whose property they are, and that hence
the one authority depends on the other, as they wish it to do.
Therefore we are now obliged to state and refute the arguments
which are rooted not in divine oracles, as were those which we
have considered, but in Roman deeds and human reason.

The first of these, which we have already mentioned, can be
put in syllogistic form, as follows: No one can hold legally what
belongs to the Church except by authority of the Church (this
is granted); the Roman government belongs to the Church;
therefore, no one can hold it legally except by authority of the
Church. The minor premise rests on the donation of Constantine, as stated. It is this minor premise which I deny, and
I shall prove that their argument for it is worthless because
Constantine could not give away the Empire, nor the Church
receive it. If they stubbornly insist on the contrary, I can prove
what I say thus: No one is permitted to do officially what is
contrary to his office, for if he were, a thing could become its contrary and still remain the same, which is impossible. No
emperor, then, is permitted to divide the empire officially, for
it is his office, as we saw in the First Book, to hold the human
race subject to a single system of approvals and disapprovals.
Hence it is not permissible for an emperor to divide the empire.

If, therefore, certain dignities were alienated, as they claim, from the Empire by Constantine, and were ceded to the Church, the seamless robe would be rent, a deed which even those dared not to do who pierced the side of Christ, the true God.

Besides, if the Church has its own foundation, so has the Empire. Now the Church's foundation is Christ; thus the Apostle writes to the Corinthians: "Other foundation no man can lay, but that which is laid, which is Christ Jesus." [20] He is the rock on which the Church is built. The Empire's foundation is human right. So I claim that, if the Church may not leave its foundation but must always rest on it, according to Canticles [of Solomon] 8:5—"Who is this that cometh up from the desert, flowing with delights, leaning upon her beloved?"—then neither may the Empire do anything contrary to human right. But to destroy itself would be an act of the Empire contrary to human right; therefore the Empire has no right to destroy itself. For it is clear that if the Empire is by its nature a universal single rule, its division would be its destruction; and that therefore no one who holds imperial authority has a right to divide the Empire. And that it is contrary to human right to destroy the Empire has already been made clear.

Besides, a jurisdiction is prior to the judge who exercises it, for the judge is appointed to the jurisdiction, not vice versa. Now the Empire is a jurisdiction embracing all temporal jurisdictions. Therefore it is prior to its judge, the emperor, because the emperor is appointed to it, not *vice versa*. Whence it is evident that the emperor may not change the Empire, for by it he is what he is. So my contention is: either Constantine, when he made the supposed donation to the Church, was emperor or he was not. If not, he clearly could not give away the Empire. If he was, he could not do such a thing as emperor, since it constituted a restriction on his jurisdiction. Moreover, if one emperor could remove even a little from the imperial jurisdiction, another could do so on the same grounds. And since all temporal jurisdiction is finite, and any finite quantity can be used up by finite subtractions, it would follow that the original jurisdiction could be annihilated, which is absurd.

[20] I Cor. 3:11.

Further, a donor is to the recipient as an agent is to the patient, according to the Philosopher in the Fourth Book of his *Nicomachean Ethics*. If a gift is to be valid, not only the donor but the recipient, too, must be suitably constituted; for though an act is *of* an agent, it appears *in* its objects and their conditions. But the Church was completely unsuited to receive temporal powers, by the express prohibition which comes to it through Matthew: "Do not possess gold, nor silver, nor money in your purses: nor scrip for your journey." [21] For, although there is some relaxation of the prohibition in Luke, I have been unable to discover any permission, subsequent to the prohibition, which would entitle the Church to own gold and silver. Wherefore if the Church was not able to receive the gift, even granted that Constantine could have made it as far as he was concerned, the act could not take place on account of the absence of a suitable recipient. It appears, therefore, that neither could the Church be a rightful possessor of the donation, nor the emperor a rightful donor, in the sense that he could alienate his own. Of course, the emperor could have entrusted to the trusteeship of the Church some of his domain and other privileges, provided he left intact his superior rule, which is indivisible. And the vicar of God could have received these not as their legal owner, but in behalf of the Church, which could distribute goods among the poor, as we know the apostles did.

11

Usurpation of a right does not create a right.

In addition, they claim that Pope Hadrian, when the Lombards under King Desiderius were oppressing him and the Church, called for the help of Charlemagne; and that it was from him that Charlemagne received the imperial dignity [and crown], even though Michael was ruling at Constantinople. On

[21] Matthew 10:9-10.

this account, they claim, all subsequent Roman emperors were not only called to the aid of the Church, but called to its aid by the Church. Hence follows the kind of dependence which they seek to prove.

To refute this, I say that they talk nonsense, because the usurpation of a right confers no right. For if it did, by the same token we could conclude that the authority of the Church comes from the emperor, since it was the Emperor Otto who restored Pope Leo, deposed Benedict, and carried him off to Saxony in exile.

12

Papal and imperial powers are different species of power and cannot be represented by one man.

Now to return to rational arguments. They assume, as their first principle, the proposition from Book X of the *Metaphysics,* which runs: All things of the same kind may be reduced to that one member of the kind which constitutes the norm of the kind. Now [they say], all men are of one kind; and therefore should be reduced to the most typical or normative man; and since pontiff and emperor are both men, they must be reduced to one. And since the pope is irreducible, they conclude that the emperor and all other men must be reduced under the pope as their norm and measure as men. Thus they arrive at the desired conclusion.

In criticizing this argument, I agree that they are right in saying that all things of the same kind should be reduced to that one which is the norm; that they are right in saying that all men are of the same kind; and that they rightly conclude that therefore all men can be reduced to the one who is norm for mankind. But when they apply this argument to pope and emperor they do so *by accident.* For one must remember that to be a man is one thing and to be pope is another, and to be emperor is still another, just as to be man, father, or lord are different kinds of being. For a man is what he is by virtue of his substantial form [or essential characteristic], in terms of which his genus and species are differentiated, and in terms of which he takes his place as a substance; but a father is what he is relatively to others of the same genus, which relation constitutes fathers a species of men not as men but in terms of another property or relation. Otherwise all distinctions could become substantial, since no relation is itself a substance, being by hypothesis a bond among substances. But such a reduction [of all relations to substantial forms] is false. Now, since pope and emperor are what they are by specific relations, that is, by the papacy and emperorship, which are themselves related to other relations, the papacy to paternity and emperorship to lordship, it is clear that as pope and emperor these two belong to different kinds and that each is reducible to the norm of its own kind. Hence I maintain that their norm as men is different from their norms as popes or emperors. For as men they belong under the best man, the measure or idea, so to speak, of all others, who would be that man who exists to a maximum degree as one of his kind. This is explained in the last books of the *Nicomachean Ethics*. But in so far as they have a relative existence, as they clearly have, they must be reduced to one either by being subordinated one to the other, or by a common relation which unites them in a species, or by some third factor which could serve as a common denominator. But neither can be said to be subordinate to the other, since the properties of either when applied to the other are false. For we do not say that the emperor is a pope, nor *vice versa*. Nor can the two be said to be members of a single species, since being pope and being emperor have very different grounds. So they must be united by means of some third relation. If we remember that things related are to each other as are their relations, and that the relations, papacy and emperorship, are relations of superiority, we can see why these two persons are of the same kind, since they are both superiors over others, and all their other qualities must be regarded as irrelevant. And this quality they have in common under God who is set above all others universally or else under some substance lower than God, but in-

cluding in its particular being all those whose particular form
of being it is to be superiors. This makes it clear that pope and
emperor are reduced to unity in one way as men, and in quite a
different way as popes and emperors. So much for their appeal
to reason.

13

*The Empire was historically prior to and independent of the
Church.*

Having stated and refuted the errors which they believe to
be their strongest arguments, who urge that the authority of
the Roman rule depends on that of the Roman pontificate, we
must now return to the more positive task of showing what the
truth is concerning this third question, with which we started
our discussion. This truth will be evident enough if we show
that the authority in question comes directly from the highest
of all beings, from God, according to the principle laid down
in the beginning of our inquiry. And we can prove this either
by eliminating the ecclesiastical authority from the question,
for no other source is even urged, or by proving clearly that
God is the immediate source of imperial authority. That the
Church is not its source can be proved thus: Anything which
may be nonexistent or inoperative without affecting the perfect functioning of another is not the cause of this other thing;
but the Church may be nonexistent or inoperative without
affecting the perfect functioning of the Empire; therefore the
Church is not a cause of the Empire's strength, and consequently not of its authority, since the authority and strength
of Empire amount to the same thing. Let A stand for the
Church, B for the Empire, and C for imperial strength or
authority. If in the absence of A, C is in B, A cannot be the
cause of C's being in B, since the being of an effect cannot pre-
cede the being of its cause. Or, if during the inactivity of A, C
is in B, it follows necessarily that A is not the cause of C's being
in B, for an effect cannot be operative before its cause, espe-

cially not before its efficient cause, which is the kind of cause now under consideration. Thus the major premise is proved to be true by an analysis of the meaning of its terms.

The minor premise is confirmed by both Christ and the Church: by Christ in his birth and death, as we explained above; by the Church when Paul said to Festus, "I stand at Caesar's judgment seat, where I ought to be judged," [22] and when God's angel said to Paul a little later, "Fear not, Paul, thou must be brought before Caesar," [23] and again when Paul afterwards said to the Jews living in Italy, "But the Jews contradicting it, I was constrained to appeal unto Caesar; not that I had aught to accuse my nation of, but that I might snatch my soul from death." [24] For, if Caesar had not then possessed the authority to judge in matters temporal, Christ would not have supported it, and the angel would not have uttered those words, and he who said, "I desire to be dissolved and to be with Christ," [25] would not have appealed to a judge without jurisdiction. And if Constantine had not possessed authority over the Church's estates, he could not have donated authoritatively what he is supposed to have given from the Empire to the Church, and hence the Church would be enjoying these grants unjustly, for God demands that all things offered to him be immaculate, as it says in Leviticus, "Every oblation which ye shall bring to the Lord shall be without leaven." [26] Though this precept is given to those who make offerings, it applies no less to those who receive them. For it would be foolish to suppose that God permits to the recipient what he prohibits to the giver, and in the same book he says explicitly to the Levites, "Pollute not your souls nor touch aught of theirs, lest ye be unclean." [27] Now it is most unfitting to declare that the Church is thus not entitled to what has been given it; and therefore the propositions on which this conclusion is based must be false.

[22] Acts 25:10.
[23] Acts 28:24.
[24] Acts 28:19.
[25] Phil. 1:23.
[26] Lev. 2:11.
[27] Lev. 2:12.

14

It is impossible that the Church could receive authority to grant temporal authority.

As to the proposition that the Church could give authority to the Roman government, it must have held this power either from God or from itself, or from some emperor, or from the universal consent of all men or at least of the greater part of them; there is no other possible source for such a power in the Church; but the Church held this power in none of these ways; therefore it did not hold it.

That none of these sources of power apply to the Church can be proved as follows: If it had received the power from God, it would have been either by divine or by natural law. (For whatever comes from nature comes from God, but not *vice versa*.) But it did not come by natural law, since nature's laws govern only nature's effects, for God, who lacks nothing, would not make anything defective when he does not use secondary agents. Now, since the Church is an effect not of nature but of God's word ("On this rock will I build my church"; and elsewhere, "I have finished the work thou gavest me to do"), it is clear that nature gave her no laws. Neither is divine law applicable here, for it is contained completely within the two Testaments, and I have found nothing within them that indicates any assignment to the priesthood, ancient or modern, of a trust or office over temporal goods. Rather I find that the ancient priests were expressly relieved of such matters, according to God's word to Moses, and the modern priests were similarly relieved by Christ's word to his disciples; but this would have been impossible had the temporal authority been derived from the priestly, since the power to authorize implies at least some care in exercising it and also a continuous vigilance to prevent the authorized persons from leaving the way of righteousness.

That the Church did not receive such power from itself is readily evident. Nothing can give what it does not have; hence the acts of any agent must be such as to show that he actually is what his actions aim at, as is explained in *Metaphysics* I. But it is clear that if the Church gave itself that power, it did not have it previously and therefore it gave itself what it did not have, which is impossible.

And that it received the power from no emperor has already been made clear enough.

And who could doubt that the power did not come through the general consent of all or most men, when not only all the Asiatics and Africans but even the greater part of Europe's inhabitants would deny such consent? Oh, it is tiresome to construct proofs, when the matter is so very clear!

15

The form of the Church is the life of Christ.

Whatever is contrary to a thing's nature is not one of its powers; for a thing's powers are according to its nature, suited to promoting its ends. But the power of authorizing the government over our mortal concerns is contrary to the Church's nature. Therefore, it is not one of its powers. As evidence for the minor premise we must be aware that in the case of the Church its nature is its form. For though nature can be attributed to either matter or form, it is more properly attributed to form, as is shown in the *Physics*. Now the form of the Church is nothing else than the life of Christ, in word and in deed. For his life was the idea and pattern of the church militant, especially of its shepherds and most especially of its chief shepherd, whose duty it is to feed the sheep and lambs. He himself said, in John's Gospel, as he bequeathed the form of his life to us, "I have given you an example that as I have done to you, so you do also." [28] And specifically to Peter, after he had assigned him the post of shepherd, he said, "Peter, follow thou me." [29] But Christ before Pilate renounced this kind of government, saying, "My kingdom is not of this world. If my kingdom were of this world,

[28] John 13:15.   [29] John 21:22.

my servants would certainly strive that I should not be delivered to the Jews; but now my kingdom is not from hence." [30] This is not to be interpreted as if Christ, who is God, were not lord of this world, for the Psalmist says, "The sea is his and he made it," but it should be interpreted as an example for the Church, which is not concerned with the rule of this world. Suppose a golden seal should say to itself, "I am not a measure at all"; it could not say this of itself as gold, for gold is the measure of all metals, but of itself as a seal which can be impressed on something else.

Accordingly the very form of the Church demands that it means what it says. To say one thing and to mean another is clearly contrary to its form, and hence to its nature, which is identical with its form. From these propositions we can deduce that it is contrary to the Church's nature to exercise the power of authorizing governments. For if a contradiction exists in opinion or speech, it arises from a contrariety in the things believed or spoken, just as truth and falsity are caused not by speech but by the things spoken. (We learn this in the doctrine of predication in the treatise, *On the Categories*.)

The above arguments are enough to prove the impropriety on the part of the Church in claiming that imperial authority depends in the slightest degree on the Church.

16

God alone rules man toward his twofold goal and chooses rulers for each.

Though in the preceding chapter we have proved, by showing the improper implications of its contrary, that the imperial authority cannot be caused by papal authority, we have not yet proved, except by implication, that this authority comes immediately from God. By implication, if it does not depend on the vicar of God, it depends on God himself. But for a perfect demonstration of our proposition it is necessary to prove that

[30] John 18:36.

the emperor or world-government derives its powers immediately from the ruler of the universe, God.

Our knowledge of this truth depends on the fact that man alone of all beings occupies a place midway between the corruptible and the incorruptible. Hence he has been rightly likened by philosophers to the horizon, which is between two hemispheres. Man has two essential parts, soul and body; considered from the point of view of one part, the body, he is corruptible; from the other, the soul, incorruptible. Of the soul the Philosopher has well stated the incorruptibility when he says, "By this alone, since it is eternal, man has achieved separation from the perishable." Accordingly, if man is a kind of mean between the corruptible and the incorruptible, like every mean, he partakes of the nature of the extremes. And since every nature is arranged to seek its proper and final goal, it follows that man exists for a double purpose. And since he alone among beings partakes of both corruptibility and incorruptibility, he alone among beings belongs in two final orders—one of which is his goal as a corruptible being, the other as incorruptible.

Twofold, therefore, are the ends which unerring Providence has ordained for man: the bliss of this life, which consists in the functioning of his own powers, and which is typified by the earthly Paradise; and the bliss of eternal life, which consists in the enjoyment of that divine vision to which he cannot attain by his own powers, except they be aided by the divine light, and this state is made intelligible by the celestial Paradise. These two states of bliss, like two different goals, man must reach by different ways. For we come to the first as we follow the philosophical teachings, applying them according to our moral and intellectual capacities; and we come to the second as we follow the spiritual teachings which transcend human reason according to our theological capacities, faith, hope, and charity. Though these two goals and their ways are made plain to us, the one by human reason, which as it is used by the philosophers makes all these things known to us, the other by the Holy Spirit, which through the prophets, through the holy

writers, through Jesus Christ the Son of God coeternal with
the Spirit, and through his disciples, has revealed to us whatever supernatural truths we need, yet man's greed would keep
them from us were not men like horses in their animal vagaries,
kept on the road by bit and rein. Thus the reins of man are
held by a double driver according to man's twofold end; one is
the supreme pontiff, who guides mankind with revelations to
life eternal, and the other is the emperor, who guides mankind
with philosophical instructions to temporal happiness. And
since none or very few (and these with difficulty) can reach
this goal, unless a free mankind enjoys the tranquillity of peace
and the waves of distracting greed are stilled, this must be the
constant aim of him who guides the globe and whom we call
Roman Prince, in order that on this threshing floor of life
mortals may exist free and in peace.

And inasmuch as the condition of our globe depends on the
order inherent in the revolving heavens, it is needful to have
the useful teachings of liberty and peace adapted to times and
places by one supervisor, to whom the total state of the heavens
is visible at once; and He alone is such a being who in his
providence sees to it that all things are ordered as he himself
has preordained. If this be the case, God alone elects, he alone
establishes governments, for he has none above him. From this
follows another conclusion, that those who now or in former
times are called Electors should not bear this title, but should
be called heralds of the divine Providence. It sometimes happens that those to whom the dignity is granted of proclaiming
the divine election fail to agree. This is because some or all of
them may have their vision clouded by the fogs of greed, so that
they cannot look into the face of the divine dispensation.

It is now clear that the authority for temporal world-government must come directly, without intermediary, from the universal Fount of authority, which, though it flows pure from a
single spring, spills over into many channels out of the abun-
dance of its goodness. And so I see that I have reached the
mark set before us. For the truth is now unfolded concerning
the basic questions in our inquiry, whether for the world's

well-being a single government must be established over it, and whether the Roman people has a right to its imperial power, and whether, lastly, the authority for world-government comes directly from God or through some other. However, the truth concerning this last question must not be interpreted so strictly as to imply that the Roman government is in no way subject to the Roman pontificate, for in some ways our mortal happiness is ordered for the sake of immortal happiness. Caesar therefore owes to Peter the piety which a first-born son owes to his father. And so, in the light of paternal grace, this government will better enlighten our globe, over which it rules through Him alone who is the ruler of all things spiritual and temporal.